AF540747

Urbanisation and Education

By

Dr. M. Lakshmi Narasaiah

M.A., Ph.D.

Professor of Economics,
Co-ordinator, Department of M.B.A. and Commerce,
Special Officer,
Sri Krishnadevaraya University Post-graduate Centre,
Kurnool–518 002
Andhra Pradesh (India)

DISCOVERY PUBLISHING HOUSE
NEW DELHI

Published by:

DISCOVERY PUBLISHING HOUSE PVT. LTD.
4383/4B, Ansari Road, Darya Ganj
New Delhi-110 002 (India)
Phone :- +91-11-23279245; 23253475; 43596065
E-mail : discoverybooksindia@gmail.com
discoverypublishinghouse@gmail.com
web : www.discoverypublishinggroup.com

***First Published:* 2006**

***Reprinted:* 2021**

ISBN: 978-81-8356-077-1

Urbanization and Education

Printed at:
Infinity Imaging Systems
Delhi

Preface

The central role of Universities in the development of skills and knowledge as an absolute prerequisite for national development is un-disputed. Higher education institutions have the responsibility for training a country's high level professional, technical and managerial personnel, they are to generate new knowledge through research and advanced scientific training, and they serve as agents in the transfer, adaptation and dissemination of knowledge. Higher education institutions also play an important role in contributing to the social cohesiveness of a nation and as a forum for constructive debates on development.

In a world economy which is heavily science-based and technology-driven higher education institutions, and particularly universities, have to provide such a competence which is indispensable for building a country's endogenous capacity for problem identification and problem solution through education combined with research. In India, however, universities have so far not been able to fulfil these roles, partly because the multiplicity of their missions is hardly compatible. Many critics of the universities in India consider them to be institutions of learning and research separated from the main stream of the economic and social needs of the population which they are supposed to serve. Most of them have not managed to reconcile the missions of providing country-oriented training and research and of being part of a wider international scientific community. Higher education institutions in many countries all over the world are confronted with a large scale and mostly uncontrolled expansion of the higher education sector and the concomitant growth expenditure against a background of dwindling financial resources to support such expansion. As a result of this expansion the quality of teaching and research has declined due to overcrowding, inadequate staffing, poor physical facilities and equipment. In addition universities often show a poor capacity for management and administration. This results in a low internal efficiency which amongst others is responsible for a rising graduate under or unemployment.

These deficiencies and a lack of national resources produce dependence on external sources particularly for research development. The low capacity for planning and management makes it difficult to properly employ external sources so that there may be pockets of good quality research in one field unrelated to neighbouring areas and not forming part of an endogenous research tradition.

Measures to be Taken

The measures may be aimed specifically at increasing the efficiency of the system of higher education or of individual institutions by improving development relevance, quality and performance. More specifically are:

- to optimise and diversify the structure in line with the country's development requirements;
- to improve the capacity for efficient planning and administration;
- to diversify funding sources, with the aim of relieving the state budget;
- to improve access for talented students from all segments of society, giving special attention to the proportion of women studying.

Dr. M. Lakshmi Narasaiah

Contents

1

Urbanisation and the Environment

Is abandoning the cities the answer to the growing ecological problems of urbanisation? The trend at any rate is in the opposite direction. At the beginning of this century, only every 10th person worldwide was a city dweller. At its end, more than half the global population will be urbanites. And most of the urban population growth will take place in the developing countries, led by Asia.

Compared to other parts of the world, however, the urbanisation process in Asia is currently not even particularly far out in front. Worldwide, city dwellers account for 43 per cent of the total population. Industrial nations have an average urbanisation rate of 72 per cent. Less industrialised countries have 34 per cent. In the Asia-Pacific region the rate is 30 per cent, in Latin America 72 per cent, and in Africa 33 per cent. The urbanisation growth rate in a number of Asian countries has in fact slowed compared with earlier years. Nevertheless, not only industrialisation, but also the increasing degree of urbanisation has emerged as a growing burden on the environment in many Asian countries.

Changed Urbanisation Pattern in India

Environment burdens are just as much a problem in the old industrial nations as they are in India. But each group has a specific pattern of development. The urbanisation process in India has proven to be more pollution-intensive than that in the old industrial nations of Europe and North America. There are several reasons for that:

- industrialisation in India is restricted to a few locations which are often concentrated in and around capital cities. Although environmental damage continues to be minor at a national level, these locations have higher pollution levels than those ever reached in Industrial nations;
- furthermore, besides the strong regionalisation of industries, the industrialisation pattern of India shows a great diversity of environmental hazards. The trend to establish "last industries first", which is promoted by progressive industrialisation, leads to a country producing certain dangerous materials before they have been covered by state regulations;
- the time factor has to be seen as an important element in the emergence of these already highly regionalised environmental burdens. In India industrialisation and its concomitant urbanisation is taking place within a ban population grew tremendously.

Growing Environmental Damage

Water pollution in India is caused mainly by domestic sewage. For example, households are responsible for 75 per cent of the pollution of the rivers. The domestic sewage problem got more and more out of control with growing urban population. Pipe-based waste water systems are rare in this country. In India dealing with waste has an extremely low priority. The type of waste disposal depends mostly on what the cities can afford. The present level of air pollution is also very high.

Innovative Approaches to Solutions

Environmental protection and economic development are seen as contradictions. Economic development can only be achieved at the cost of higher levels of environmental pollution. And in reverse, if pollution is to be controlled and reduced this can only be done to the disadvantage of further development. In the meantime, however, numerous instances of successful urban environmental management are developing. They could help to change and subsequently break through the existing pattern of thinking. The following approaches can be viewed as important.

Combining regulations with incentives: The introduction of lead-free petrol and the mandatory equipping of new cars with catalytic converters is still by no means common in India. As numerous cars without catalytic converters are still able to use lead-free. Converters were then at first made compulsory for higher-powered cars, and later also for compact models.

Combining regulations with simple controls: Apart from general limitation of the number of cars in the city, its most important single measure to prevent traffic jams and the additional petrol consumption and pollutant emissions caused by them.

High economic growth in India has in fact led to a general reduction of poverty. But the distribution of income, particularly between urban and rural areas, has remained relatively constant. Urban environmental and traffic problems have increased heavily during the same period. These developments can be attributed to a certain pattern of official action (or "non-action"):

- governments have made efforts in supplying roads, but neglected the demand for mobility;
- governments are preoccupied with supplying water, and have neglected follow up problems, above all the questions of waste water disposal and treatment. In Indian cities, for example, this leads to the absurd situation that due to the mushroom-like growth of the cities and the increased water pollution linked with it, water must be brought in over ever greater distances and at ever greater expense;
- governments take a one-sided look at noxious substances. Concentrations of harmful substances in

water and in the air are in fact checked, and some measures are taken against individual pollutants of single sectors (e.g. lead emissions by the transport sector).

But an integrated policy which operates integrated environmental management with the aim of comprehensively relieving the burdens on the environment has not yet been developed anywhere. To consider such a concept, it is necessary to cut loose from the customary way of approaching problems. It makes sense not to separate the problem areas from each other according to sectors and pollutants, but rather on the basis of their ecological impact.

Orienting on demand hits the core of the concept of ecological modernisation, which is about reducing the intensity of resource use (note, at this stage this does not yet mean the absolute reduction of inputs). At the same time, sights are set on a lower use of land with the same size of population, or also lower energy consumption with the same degree of added value or the same per capita income.

Finally, the importance of governments for creating framework conditions must be emphasised once again. Because the actors come from different spheres, such conditions are essential.

From the time of the Greek polis, it was the ambition of the Greek city councillors to pass on a city that was more beautiful than the one they had taken over. There is a long way to go before such an attribute asserts itself in India (and elsewhere).

2

Urbanisation and Globalisation

How we handle globalisation will determine whether our cities and our civilisation will be divided and violent or user-friendly and peaceful. We cannot get a clear picture of urban life in the 21st century, especially in the poor countries of the South, unless we take into account the phenomenon of globalisation, which has already brought dramatic changes make their first appearance. So it is there too that the great upheavals of the next century will take place.

Globalisation given shape to the "Global Village". The "information era" that it ushers in compresses time and we are now living in a world speeded up as never before. Worldwide urbanisation is proceeding at a similar rate and its pace in the poor countries of the South seems terrifying. By 2025, two-thirds of humanity will be living in cities and towns, where the best opportunities in life tend to be.

Globalisation also accentuates a "new urban geography" in both North and South. Islands of rich consumers are springing up in cities amid an ocean of deprived people. More and more unemployed people, immigrants, minorities and the homeless, are pushed into cities by pressure from "market economies". As a result, all urban area—not just those in the poor countries of the South—will have to deal with growing internal tensions. In New York, for example, the poorest 20 per cent of the population earns 15 times less than the richest 20 per cent.

Cities have always had their smart neighbourhoods and their dangerous areas. But such social and geographical segregation has changed in pace and scale because of the growth in the urban population, the increase in "illegal" migrants and rising uncertainty.

In fact, we have entered a period of historical transition, where discontinuities prevail over adjustment. Radical changes in the nature of production and jobs and the incredible concentration of capital in the hands of the financial sector and speculators weigh much heavier in our lives these days than the state's efforts to adjust and improve the market economy. Segregation in cities has been given a new lease of life whose consequences we do not know. It has reached unprecedented dimensions because of the explosive growth of urban areas.

According to one scenario, things will go badly. The growing pace of globalisation will increase uncertainty about the future. Fear and defence mechanisms will grow among people and institutions, fuelling intolerance, xenophobia and mistrust of everything new or foreign. Urban tensions will manifest themselves with increasing violence, and segregation will sharpen. Public areas will be abandoned and become dangerous no-man's lands, the wretched abode of society's rejects. Cities will lose their original function of being a crossroads for meeting and exchange.

If globalisation also continues to go hand in hand with deregulation of financial markets and an unchanged level of indebtedness of poor countries, the latter will not be able to maintain their urban infrastructures. And if on top of this there is corruption and lack of political will, challenges to the system will increase and violence will grow. Cash-strapped authorities will respond with undemocratic mafias which provide them with funds.

According to a second scenario, everything will be all right. In line with the principle that "everything the state does is public, but the state doesn't control everything that is public," a new social contract will be drawn up between the state, the market, the working population and civil society, including NGOs. Cities will develop a new quality of life by providing citizens with forum for exchange. Jobs will be created in the social sector, in the fields of the environment, education, research, culture and leisure, opening up possibilities for young people.

In the countries of the South, long-term development strategies will be drafted and urban planning practised, taking advantage of the opportunities provided by globalisation but without falling into its traps. Town planning will become part of the political process, and the state will work with the private sector, monitored by institutions of civil society. Adequate housing will be built with the help of micro-credit and controls on the price of building materials. Improved infrastructures will enable marginal areas to become part of the civilised part of the city. Democracy will come up with new ways of governing with the help of networks of involved citizens.

In a transitional scenario, action strategies should fall somewhere between these two extremes. They should include social goals so that in big urban areas a society emerges which is founded on participatory democracy and on "capitalism with a human face" or "market socialism".

But the outlook is less clear than ever. Let us hope the present transition will lead rapidly to a new revival of humanism, whose first signs we are already seeing. This would open up the road to a development which is fair, humane and peaceful.

3

Population Growth and Urbanisation

The world's cities are growing far faster than its population. Indeed, aside from the growth of population itself, urbanisation is the dominant demographic trend of the half-century now ending. In 1950, 750 million of the world's people lived in cities. By 1996, this had at least tripled, to more than 2.6 billion. The number projected to live in cities by 2050, some 6.5 billion people, exceeds world population today.

Urbanisation on anything like the scale that we know today is historically quite recent. In 1800, only one city, London, had a million people. Today, 326 cities have at least that many people. And there are 14 mega cities, those with 10 million or more residents. Tokyo is the largest, at 27 million. Mexico city is second, at 17 million. New York city and Sao Paulo are close behind, with 16 million each. Rounding out the list in descending size are Bombay (15 million), Shanghai (14), Los Angeles (12), Calcutta (12), Buenos Aires (12), Beijing (11), Osaka (11), Lagos (10), Rio de Janeiro (10), and Delhi (10).

The rate of growth of cities in industrial countries during the first century or so of the Industrial Revolution was relatively slow. Today's cities are growing much faster. It took London 130 years to get from 1 million to 8 million. Mexico city made this jump in just 30 years.

Measured in annual growth, some cities, such as Lagos, Nigeria, are growing at 5 per cent a year; Bombay is growing at nearly 4 per cent. The world's urban population as a whole is growing by just over 1 million people each week. This urban growth is fed by natural increase of urban populations, by net migration from the countryside, and by villages, by net migration from the countryside, and by villages or towns expanding to the point where they become cities or they are absorbed by the spread of existing cities.

During the early stages of industrialisation, urbanisation was largely in response to the pull of employment opportunities in cities. More recently, however, the movement from countryside to city has been more the result of rural push than of urban pull. It is a reflection of the lack of opportunity in the countryside as already small plots of land are divided and then divided again with each passing generation, until they become so small that people can no longer make a living from them.

Historically, cities and the surrounding countryside had a symbolic relationship, with the latter supplying food and raw materials in exchange for manufactured products. Today, cities are tied much more to each other and to the global economy. The food and fuel that once came from the surrounding countryside now often comes from distant corners of the planet.

As societies urbanize, the use of basic resources, such an energy and water rises. In traditional rural societies, for example, people live on the land and thus do not need to travel to work. But once they migrate to cities, commuting becomes the rule, not the exception. In villages, most of the food that is consumed is produced locally, requiring little energy for processing, packaging, and transportation; once people move into cities, on the other hand, virtually all their food must be brought in. In a village where residents typically draw their water from a central well and carry it to their homes, water use in necessarily limited. But when villagers move to urban high-rise apartment buildings with indoor plumbing, replete with showers and flush toilets, water consumption soars.

The ecology of cities is a continuing challenge to city managers simply because cities require the concentration of huge quantities of water, food, energy and raw materials. The waste products must then be dispersed or the city will become uninhabitable. As cities become larger, the disposal of residential and industrial wastes becomes ever more challenging.

Partly as a result of the mounting pressure for people to migrate to cities, the growth in urban populations is far out-stripping the availability of basic services, such as water, sewerage, transportation, and electricity. As a result, life in urban shantytowns is plagued by poverty, pollution, congestion, homelessness, and unemployment.

Since the beginning of the Industrial Revolution, the terms of trade between countryside and city have favored the latter simply because cities control the scarce resources in development, namely capital and technology. But if the price of food rises in the years ahead, as now seems likely, the terms of trade could shift, favoring the countryside. If in the new world of the twenty-first century the scarce resources are land and water, those controlling them could have the upper hand in determining rural/urban terms of trade.

This aside, if recent trends continue, within the next several years more than half of us will be living in cities—making the world more urban than rural for the first time in history. We will have become an urban species, far removed from our hunter-gatherer origins.

4

In Defence of the City Urban Development a Key for Survival

The figures sound alarming. The towns and cities in developing countries are growing faster than ever before. By the year 2000, 2.2 billion people will live in the cities of the Third World. Their numbers are expected to double by the year 2025. But many of the cities in Africa, Asia and Latin America are already bursting at the seams. Some of the so-called megacities have more than 10 or 15 million inhabitants. Many of them live in unplanned squatter settlements, without water and electricity, in an environment of squalor, poverty, crime and disease. Nevertheless, the cities seem to have lost nothing of their attraction for the rural populations. Although the larger share of the population increase in the cities of developing countries is caused by the children of people already living there, the rural-urban migration continues unabated. The cities still offer better chances for employment and education, they provide a better physical infrastructure, better health facilities and a more interesting life. Miserable as conditions in the cities often appear to be, they are usually much better than those in the rural areas. It is, therefore, an illusion to believe that the growth of the cities could be checked by concentrating the development efforts on the countryside. There is no alternative to urban development in a world will soon count some 8 billion people.

Cities have always been in the vanguard of development. The ancient civilisations of Mesopotamia,

Egypt, Greece and Rome were city cultures which for the first time in human development created large, well-governed states. In Europe during the Middle Ages, the creation of towns and cities offered the rural populations a chance to evade the oppression by feudal authorities and become free citizens. Local self-government in medieval towns is at the cradle of democratic development. There is a clear separation of competence between the national, state and local level of government leaving citizens an opportunity to decide on matters which directly affect their own local environment. It is worth looking at this model when discussing ways organised to improve city governance and allow for more participation of the population.

Another fact worth looking at is the size of cities in Industrialised countries. Although about three quarters of the people live in urban areas, there are only a handful of really big cities.

Of course, the growth of towns and cities in developed countries is the result of a long historical process, deeply rooted in the particular political and economic conditions of the past centuries. In developing countries today, other conditions prevail which favour the emergence of ever bigger urban conglomerations. However, governments are able, thorough appropriate investments and the location of industries educational facilities or housing policies to influence the settlement trends in their respective countries in favour of smaller cities.

One point seems certain, though, when considering the pros and cons of city development: the severe environmental problems facing mankind today can only be solved if people live in highly concentrated settlements rather than being spread out evenly over the whole countryside. Environment-friendly mass transport, for instance, is only possible in the cities. Fossil fuel consumption which adds to the pollution of the atmosphere will be lower when people live close to their places of work. Their supply with food, water, electricity and social amenities is cheaper and uses up fewer resources when distances are short. The use of land for housing, transport and industry is less when buildings grow in height rather than space. Even refuse disposal and wastewater management is easier to organise in a big city than in the countryside.

What is important then is not to question the validity of city development, but to make cities and tows a better place to live in. Good city governance, more involvement of the population in decision-making, more attention paid to environmental hazards caused by congestion and low safety standards are some of the demands that must be met to cope with the problems of the cities. There is no reason to bedevil the city as the most successful form of human settlement. Since the times of Babylon, it has also been a place where many different peoples and cultures meet. A generation from now, half the human population will live in cities. We should see this as a chance for human survival.

5

Urbanisation in India and Limitations

Urban growth is an undeniable fact of the future in India. Only 1 in 10 people lived in cities when this century began; nearly half will by the century's end. Urban migration accounts for a large share of this rapid growth. Upto 60 per cent of the people in many cities in India live in burgeoning, impoverished squatter settlements.

Allowing urban development to spread out upon undisturbed land exacerbates automobile dependence and destroys the natural environment. Yet it is impossible to truly halt development; prohibiting growth in one jurisdiction merely shifts it to neighbouring areas. The key to a livable and viable future for the India's urban areas is neither to encourage sprawled growth nor to try to stifle growth altogether—but rather, to encourage compact growth.

Forward-looking Municipalities have discovered that compact development can accommodate expanding populations without despoiling the surrounding environment. These cities are actually using urban growth to their advantage: for example, compact development, by making public transit, cycling, and walking more practical, reduces reliance on cars so that less energy is used and less pollution generated. Filling in their under-used space has allowed these cities to become more pleasant and convenient places to live. With less space paved over for parking lots and urban highways, more room is available for homes, workplaces, and green space.

In the long run, population stabilisation—via more effective family planning and elimination of poverty—is essential to the future of the Indian cities. But it will take decades to stabilise population growth. In the mean time it is essential for urban areas to begin redesigning themselves. With compact development, urban areas can meet people's expanding needs by making the most of existing space.

Somewhere to Grow

Many cities have so much underused space that they could develop for decades to come without bulldozing another square yard of undisturbed land. Although much underuse of property results from individuals and companies holding it for speculation, local governments themselves frequently hold large amounts of vacant real estate. Surplus government buildings and other public holdings often stay idle while growth mushrooms a the city's edge. In India great potential for filling in underused space lies in redistributing urban land ownership. Land reform, granted, is among the most difficult political moves a government can undertake, Yet the need for such an effort is difficult to deny.

Cities have tremendous scope for making urban growth more compact by establishing urban growth boundaries outside of which further development is prohibited. Greenbelts surrounding cities perform this function in India. Cities of strict land-use planning charge that urban growth boundaries and other bold measures encroach on individual freedoms. Yet guiding development more rationally can in fact do more to protect people's rights, while keeping cities livable.

Urban Density: The Real Story

Often, people move out to the suburbs seeking open space and bonds with nature that come only in a rural setting. Yet most of these residents continue to maintain an urban life style—commuting to jobs in the city and demanding an assortment of urban amenities found in suburban shopping malls. The result is neither urban nor rural living, but a destructive compromise that the environment cannot sustain.

The low-density suburban model not only has come at a high ecological price, but it also has failed to deliver on many of its promises. Seeking freedom, mobility, fresh air and access to open space, many suburbanites instead encounter long commutes and traffic jams caused by the dispersed communities' nearly exclusive reliance on private automobiles. Suburban life promises escape from crime in the city, only to trade that danger for the far greater chance of being injured or killed in a car accident. And a new form of social inequity has emerged, stranding anyone who cannot drive or afford a car.

Although denser land use could help solve the environmental, social and aesthetic problems of sprawl, widespread misconceptions about increased density—even moderate density—often prevent communities from adopting compact land use strategies. Contrary to popular belief, augmenting the density of development does not create a harsh physical environment. Planners and citizens, often assume that moderate and high-density land use are synonymous with crime, poverty and squalor. Yet there is no scientific evidence to support a direct link between these social problems and density.

Transport's Missing Link

One of the most destructive by products of low-density sprawl is an automobile-dependent transport system. The pattern of urban development dictates whether people can walk or cycle to work or whether they need to travel dozens of miles; it also determines whether a new bus or rail line can attract enough riders. Despite this obvious link, city layouts often are too dispersed to foster efficient transportation. Many of the India's cities have failed to implement compact land use as a transport strategy; few foresaw that an automobile orientation would later plague them with traffic jams, deadly accidents, harmful noise and smog, while marginalising people who do not own cars. A more rational approach for Indian cities would be to integrate homes not only with workplaces but with commercial, recreational and other land uses so they are easily accessible without cars. Such reforms ideally would not hamper developers or impose uniformity, but instead would lift restriction that create unnaturally one-dimensional districts.

The key to making integrated zoning work well as a transport strategy is to encourage urban development that is dense enough to promote alternatives to cars. For example, transport planners estimate that an Indian city typically requires at least seven dwellings per acre in a given area to support reasonably frequent local bus service, nine dwellings for light rail and 15 dwellings for an express bus. These moderate densities can be reached by mingling clusters of single-family homes with garden apartments and two-to six-story apartment buildings.

Many large cities are finding that the most transport-efficient land use pattern combines a compact, well-mixed downtown with several outlying, high-density areas—all linked by an extensive public transport system. This way, people can walk, cycle and take short public transport trips within a given area and reach other areas via express bus or rapid light rail.

Room Enough for All

Attempts to slow or stop growth shut out many groups of people—and by restricting the supply of housing, tend to inflate home prices. Compact growth, by contrast, can help create diverse communities and promote smaller, more affordable housing.

Cities of India can combine compact growth with strategies to increase the supply of land available for low and moderate-income homes. India can made use of measures to prevent speculation, a process whereby land owners in nearly all free-market societies hold land as an investment for future wind-fall gains, rather than putting it to current use. Speculation puts upward pressure on real estate prices and idles great amounts of urban land.

By taxing vacant land according to its true worth in the market, cities can make these parcels less attractive as an investment vehicle. Local governments typically assess such properties at far less than their market value, effectively rewarding property owners for keeping their land idle. More accurate property assessment encourages redevelopment. Cities can go a step further to tax vacant land more heavily than developed parcels. To avoid spurts of sprawled growth, however, it is critically important to combine these tax strategies with clearly defined growth frontiers—such as greenbelts and urban growth boundaries—that contain development within the existing urban area.

Municipalities can enhance the supply of affordable housing require each house to occupy its own spacious lot with controls that promote a variety of housing types, including smaller and multi-family homes.

A more immediate remedy to the housing crunch felt in many cities, where homes tend to be large, is to allow single-family home owners to rent out small apartments within their homes. The size of the average household is shrinking steadily as couples have fewer children and more people choose living arrangements other than the nuclear family. As a result, many homes built for larger households can create an extra unit in a converted basement, garage, attic or even an added story.

Laying the Groundwork

Creating compact cities requires a commitment by planning authorities and governments at the local, regional and national levels. Adequate local planning institutions are especially lacking in the developing world. Municipal government in India often have neither the authority to guide land use nor the funds to provide basic services. With few exceptions, urban planning is a relatively recent phenomenon in India.

Compact growth of cities also hinges on regional cooperation, an important tool for handling conflicts between the interests of individual localities and those of the broader region. All cities in India are required to plan their own development according to stipulated goals, such as energy conservation, protection of open space and provision of affordable housing. These statewide planning requirements not only enhance regional cooperation, but they also give cities the backing they need to apply a comprehensive, long-term vision to their land use planning.

Finally, the effectiveness of urban planning can be fully achieved only if governments remove the conflicting incentives posed by other national policies. Among the greatest barriers to compact urban development are artificially low petrol prices, which encourage dependence on cars.

If the barriers to efficient land use were removed, what would a compact city look like? Much of the vast space normally devoted to automobile parking in a sprawled, car-dependent city would be planted in trees and flowers, or used for building homes. Old properties would be revived for new uses; a 19th century warehouse into apartments, a vacant lot into a public park, for instance, the downtown area would be lived in day and night, with apartments and offices occupying the floors above ground-level shops. Each district would be home to a variety of jobs, shops and day care centres, all within an easy walk or bicycle ride. People could travel quickly to other parts of the city and outlying areas via rapid rail and express bus lines.

On a rapidly urbanising India, societies can take greater command of their fate by more consciously determining the use of urban land. Whether surrounded by affluent suburbs or makeshift shantytowns, the cities can protect the environment and better address the needs of current and future generations by planning for compact growth.

6

Land Tenure

Securing Land for the Urban Poor

Around the world, especially in Asia and Africa, towns and cities are expanding rapidly. For the poorest people, finding affordable, safe and secure urban land for shelter has become increasingly difficult. This is because:

- Overall competition for land makes it increasingly costly;
- Central urban areas are being developed for commercial use;
- Natural features such as mountains or swamps limit physical urban expansion; and
- Meeting land management and planning standards (concerned with legality, technical and administrative accuracy) is expensive.

As a result, a large and increasing proportion of urban populations are forced to live in peripheral areas or occupy marginalised and dangerous locations. These settlements are often illegal and, providing inadequate shelter and lacking essential services, only exacerbate the problems of the poor. Higher levels of ill health, unemployment and non-sustainable land-use often result. Furthermore, residents may also be under constant threat of eviction by government and exploitation by landowners.

Experience shows that, if residents in such areas feel secure and safe from eviction, they do over time, improve their neighbourhoods. Recognition of and granting of secure forms of tenure to previously illegal settlements often provides the incentive to communities to invest their resources in upgrading their housing and wider neighbourhoods. Security of tenure also brings the improved likelihood of basic infrastructure and other essential community services.

There is a wide range of urban land tenure systems. In many urban areas, including areas designated illegal by government, there are informal or customary tenure systems—these are often the commonest form of tenure and are expanding most rapidly.

While statutory or "legal" forms of tenure (for example freehold or leasehold agreements) offer many advantages, such as full individual rights and security and access to formal credit systems, they can also cause the very problems they were intended to solve:

- Higher rental levels, which may displace existing renters;
- The selling out of the secure land to higher income groups;
- Encouragement of new illegal/informal settlements, as the poorest hope that they will also eventually get security of tenure;
- Encouragement of landowners and developers to hold land, without investing in its improvement or paying taxes on its increased value—which serves to attract even greater levels of investment and land price inflation.

In addition, if peoples' income remain low and the capacity of the banks or credit unions is weak, statutory forms of tenure alone may not necessarily stimulate neighbourhood improvements.

Consequently, careful analysis of existing systems of informal and customary tenure and property right is required, before embarking on major land management and tenure reforms. These can provide both acceptable levels of security and access to credit, which in turn stimulate improvements to local neighbourhoods. Before any decisions are made, tenure policies must recognise the likely impact on tenants, the poor and other vulnerable groups, especially women.

For these reasons, it is sometimes better to increase the rights of residents (e.g. by protecting them from the threat of forced evictions, or by increasing their access to essential utilities or credit), rather than assuming that they need freehold or leasehold titles.

Strategies for providing shelter now recognise the diverse nature of needs and the positive contribution which decent housing makes to social and economic development at both national and local levels. They also recognise that the most effective way of mobilising the resources required is to encourage investment in housing by individuals, communities and the private sector.

Recent experience shows that many governments are now introducing positive approaches, which are market-sensitive and encourage more efficient use of available land. These include measures to encourage landowners and developers to allocate a specified proportion of units to low-income groups out of profits generated from planning permission granted by (and therefore partly created by) the government. Public-private partnerships and revisions to planning standards and administrative procedures have also demonstrated that it is possible to reduce the costs of access to land for the poor even under conditions of market-led development, thus reducing urban sprawl, the occurrence of slum settlements and levels of poverty.

7

Towards Healthy Cities

More than a third of the urban population in developing world live in housing of such poor quality with such inadequate provision for water, sanitation, drainage, garbage collection and health care that their health is constantly under threat. But, properly planned, cities can be safe and healthy.

In the cities of India, it is common for one child in three to die before the age of five and for virtually all infants, children and adults who survive to have disease burdens many times higher than they should.

Diarrhoea, tuberculosis and respiratory infections (each among the largest causes of death) are generally much increased by over-crowding. Many accidental injuries happen when there are three or more persons living in each small room in shelters made of flammable materials and there is little chance of providing occupants (especially children) with protection from open fires or stoves.

But cities also include some of the India's safest and most healthy neighbourhoods. High densities allow much lower costs for supplying each household with piped, treated water supplies and most forms of health, educational and emergency services.

Sanitation and drainage may be costly in cities, as complex systems are needed to cope with high densities and large population concentrations but city households can generally afford to pay more—and are prepared to do so if they get a good service.

Cities may be considered ecologically unsustainable because of high consumption and waste levels but well planned and managed cities can combine high living standards with remarkably low levels of energy consumption, resource use and wastes. The concentration of people and production creates many more possibilities of collecting and recycling wastes and for walking, bicycling and a high quality public transport.

For many, city life is one of excessive workloads and drudgery, yet cities remain centres of culture—including the visual and decorative arts, music, dance, theatre and literature. Most cities have a large reserve of young people on whose initiative and energy they could draw to improve condition—yet most such people find that their cities offer them little hope and little prospect of employment. If cities have such potential to provide healthy, stimulating and valued places to live and work for all age groups, why do so few achieve this?

Supporting Change

Much of the explanation is the lack of 'good governance'. Good governance in any city means encouragement and support from all levels of government for a great range of investments of capital, expertise and time by individuals, households, communities, voluntary organisations and NGOs—as well as private enterprises. In most cities in India, the total value of investments made by people in their own homes and neighbourhoods exceeds many times the total value of capital investments made by city and municipal authorities. Yet governments and aid agencies usually ignore (or deem illegal) most such efforts.

Most households who want their own home cannot afford to purchase one—or at least one that is legal. They cannot obtain housing loans so the cost of the house purchase can be spread over a number of years—as they cannot meet the (usually) inappropriate conditions set by banks or housing finance institutions. If they turn to building their own home—as most do—they have to occupy or purchase the site illegally. They often have to build on dangerous sites—in floodplains or on slopes with frequent landslides or mudslides—as the cost of safer sites is too high.

Even if they can qualify, for a housing loan, most such loans are for finished houses, not for incremental construction. And even when they have developed their own home and neighbourhood into a viable residential area, governments usually refuse to provide these with roads, water supplies, drains and other essential infrastructure, because they are 'illegal'

What would cities look like today if governments had supported these individual and community efforts by ensuring that land, building materials, credit and technical advice were as cheap and readily available as possible? Or if government-community partnerships had been formed to, at least, improve water supply, sanitation, drainage and health care.

These work within what is often called the 'social economy'—the great variety of initiatives and actions that are organised and controlled locally and that are not profit-oriented. The social economy includes the work of citizen groups, resident's associations, street or barrio clubs, youth clubs and parent associations that support local schools. It includes many voluntary groups that provide services for the elderly, the physically disabled or other individuals in need of social. It often includes many initiatives that make cities safer and more fun helping provide supervised play space, sport and recreational opportunities for children and youth. It may provide formal or informal supervision or maintenance of parks, squares and other public spaces.

The social economy not only 'gets things done' but also creates a dense fabric of relationships that allows citizens to work together in identifying and acting on local problems.

Its value to a 'healthy city' is enormous, even if it is often forgotten by governments and international agencies.

The capacity of city authorities to govern is not the same as the capacity to invest, since these authorities can do much to encourage and support the social economy. City authorities can often greatly increase the supply and reduce the cost of land for housing by changing inappropriate regulations, streamlining planning and land use control, procedure and making better use of publicly owned land.

City authorities should also have the main role in enforcing legislation on air and water pollution and occupational health and safety. This does not require large investments by public authorities, but it can do much to improve health and the quality of life in a city. Good governance also means managing competing claims and finding common ground between enterprises, trade unions and residents about what should be done to make the city more healthy.

Achieving a healthy city needs a representative political system through which the priorities of citizens and businesses can influence policies and actions. Democratic structures remain among the best checks on the misallocation of resources by city and municipal governments. Actively involving a wide range of local groups in developing 'city governance' helps ensure that the different priorities of a wide range of groups are addressed.

The key issue is not so much identifying what should be done to achieve more healthy cities. This is well known. It is identifying how it should be done, especially how governments and international agencies can support a vast range of activities by individuals, households and communities that help build and maintain healthy cities—which to date they have ignored or even (for many governments) repressed.

8

Sustainable Cities

Today almost one half of the world's population lives in cities. The world's cities are growing by one million people each week. Cities today play a significant role in development. They continue to attract migrants from rural areas because they enable people to advance socially and economically. Cities offer significant economies of scale in the provision of jobs, housing and services and are important centres of productivity and social development.

However, the stress of this rapid urban population growth is often overwhelming. The long list of afflictions includes urban poverty rates of up to 60 per cent. Despite growing investments, more than one third of the urban population live in substandard housing. Forty per cent of urban dwellers do not have access to safe drinking water or adequate sanitation. Primarily due to a rapid growth and a deteriorating urban environment, at least 600 million people in human settlements (cities, towns and villages) already live in health and life-threatening situations, and almost 50 per cent of these are children.

The high rate of urban population growth in most regions has led to common problems: congestion, lack of funds to provide basic services, a shortage of adequate housing and declining infrastructure, to name a few.

While these problems are occurring in urban areas, cities still have an important role to play in protecting the global environment in the face of rapid urban population growth. Agricultural and livestock production in rural areas are pushing farther and farther into ecologically fragile regions and cannot support growing population. The finite land and water resources make it imperative that human settlements be carefully planned. Indeed, sustainable urbanisation will ease the pressures caused by encroachment on fragile natural habitats.

India's cities offer a bewildering sight to any visitor: the congestion caused by rapid population growth and a continuing rural-urban drift often leads to conditions which defy all rules of orders, hygiene and environmental safety. Inadequate leadership, corruption and mismanagement have a harmful effect on the physical, environmental, social and ethical structures of cities in India.

Millions of people live in inadequate conditions—without piped water, electricity, security of land tenure, access to roads or health facilities. The means available for production and financing of housing and urban infrastructure are too limited to meet basic needs.

Reducing Poverty and Creating Jobs

Urban poverty is rising at an alarming pace, especially among women. The informal economic sector—which makes a substantial contribution to the delivery of services, production of goods, building of infrastructure and housing construction—often provides the only opportunity for the urban poor to make a living.

Local informal housing construction, for example, generates up to 20 per cent more jobs than high-cost construction. Street hawking, waste recycling and food production are primary sources of income among the urban poor and are illustrative of the creativity of survival strategies.

However, the informal sector itself is often highly exploitative and fails to raise people's economic development beyond mere subsistence. Larger economic strategies and more participatory urban planning approaches that take stock of local skills, technologies and materials are required to generate new and better-paying job opportunities in cities and towns.

Incorporating Environmental Concerns

In 1992 the Rio Conference on Environment and Development designed the Agenda 21 Programme of Action to help save a planet endangered by environmental neglect and plagued by poverty and underdevelopment. Most of the goals agreed to in Rio can become reality only through local action in cities where environmental threats are increasing. Again, it is the urban poor who are particularly endangered by environmental degradation and pollution. The world's Agenda 21 will fail if the city's environmental agenda (population, inadequate sanitation, water supply and waste management) is not addressed. This is being recognised by local authorities all over the world.

Sustainable development in the twenty first century will to a large degree, depend upon how cities, towns and villages everywhere interact with the environment and utilize natural resources.

Increasing Awareness of Gender Issues

Women and men use and experience cities differently, according to their roles, responsibilities and access to resources. For example, when basic services are lacking in a settlement, more often than not it is women who take on responsibilities such as water collection and refuse disposal. Women often have unequal access to resources such as property, credit, training and technology. All of these factors must be addressed urgently, as they make it harder for women to improve their living standards and those of their children.

Disaster Mitigation Relief and Reconstruction

As cities become large and more densely populated, they become increasingly vulnerable to natural and man-made disasters such as earthquake, floods, industrial hazards, epidemics, civil strife and wars. Poor people are forced to live in the most exposed, dangerous and cramped conditions; in flood-prone areas, on steep hillsides or near polluted streams and waste dumps. As a result, they are most likely to lose their homes or their lives when disasters occur. Better planning, access to affordable urban land and improved construction methods can reduce the extent of catastrophes.

These successful and sustainable approaches to poverty eradication; managing the urban environment; providing access to land, shelter and finance; empowering women and men; and many other issues will have to be documented and disseminated widely.

9

Living with Leviathan

In the year 2015, there will mega-cities with more than 8 million inhabitants—22 of them in Asia. How will they cope? Humanity is about to set a new record. Nearly two-thirds of the planet's population will be living in cities by 2025, UN population experts say. Until now, rural people have outnumbered city-dwellers.

World population, according to the same projections, will top eight billion in 25 year's time, including five billion in cities. The increase will be particularly spectacular in the cities of the developing world, whose total population will double to four billion. We are going to see an unprecedented exodus of people from rural areas.

The demographer's predictions are only tentative of course. But the flow of people into megacities in developing countries is well under way. Several sociological changes are behind it.

Cities used to need muscle power for the jobs they provided, the experts point out. But today they no longer attract people just because of their economic potential. There is plenty of evidence that they can go on steadily attracting people even when the job-generating sectors are in bad shape or disappearing.

People no longer move to urban centers because they are fairly sure to find work. They do so because thcy want to leave the countryside where there are too many people tilling the land and because they hope to leave poverty behind. Rightly or wrongly, the city seems to offer progress and freedom, a vision of opportunity, an irresistible lure.

The result is that both inside and outside cities, there are more and more squatters and poor housing. Urbanisation in the developing world differs from that in the industrialised countries, in "the speed of the process, the growth of poverty, the extent of urban sprawl and the expansion of the informal economy."

How are the authorities in the developing world's urban areas responding to such "invasions"? In today's deregulated world, the trend is to question the very idea of providing the general population with basic urban services, most observers note. For want of resources, cities in developing countries are increasingly abandoning their public service function.

China is still an exception to this in several ways. Officials there, in a context of rigid planning—though this has eased in recent years—are trying to prevent the influx of more rural migrants than the city economies can cope with, as the example of Shanghai shows. Can such a policy, which works fairly well for the moment, survive the political and economic hangs under way?

At the other end of the scale is Lagos (Nigeria), whose expansion is chaotic, about 200 slums have sprung up in this African city. Every now and then, one of them is bulldozed without notice and without heed for its inhabitants. But Lagos survives, thanks to the vibrant ingenuity of its millions of citizens. Another revealing city is Jakarta, where the authorities themselves have joined in frantic property speculation. As a result of this speculation, more than 4.5 million people have been evicted from their homes in the last 30 years, with little compensation, to make possible the construction of high-rise blocks, which sometimes stand empty.

How do the original inhabitants of a city react to the massive influx of people from outside? In more and more cities, you see smart neighbourhoods protected by guards—called "fortress-cities". In these fortified enclaves, built partly in response to real or imagined lack of security, the roads, sewage system, schools and other community services are private. Outside them, public areas have been abandoned to the least fortunate members of the society and the infrastructure there is crumbling or inadequate. The middle and poorer classes also defend themselves in their own neighbourhoods. One surprising case can be found in the satellite cities just outside Brasilia, where iron railing protect the houses, from fancy villas to the humblest shack.

Will the mega-cities of the 21st century be made up of island of "social tribes"- "anticities" of walled enclaves, whose wealthy residents refuse to pay taxes to provide facilities for the city's less fortunate inhabitants? Will cities still integrate their inhabitants?

"The existence of a slum means the authorities have failed," says the World Bank. The bank encourages projects where the state and the private sector join hands to help the less fortunate buy plots of land in areas with an infrastructure. Other experts say the "anti-social" aspects of globalisation should be blamed. They would like to see the big cities of the next century return to their original function as a crossroads and a meeting-place.

10

Cities at the Forefront

The rapid growth of cities in the developing world puts them in the forefront of the struggle for improved living standards and protection of the environment. Since 1950 the urban population has more than tripled, from just over 750 million to about 3 billion. By 2030 some 5 billion people will live in cities. In the developing world the urban population is projected to double from 1.9 billion in 2000 to be just under 4 billion by 2030.

Worldwide, about three fourths of all current population growth is urban. Cities are gaining an estimated 55 million people per year—over 1 million new residents every week from in-migration and natural population increase within cities. In developing countries many cities are growing two or three times faster than population growth for the country as a whole. As cities grow ever lager, their impact on the environment grows exponentially.

The Rise of Megacities

The UN coined the term megacities in 1970s to describe cities with 10 million or more residents. As recently as 1975 there were only five megacities worldwide. Currently, there are 19 megacities, of which 15 are in developing countries. By 2015 the number of megacities will grow to 23 which is explained in Table 10.1. Megacities have captured public interest because cities this large are unprecedented in history and because of the popular perception that human well-being will decline in such dense concentration of people.

Millions of people move from the countryside to the city to seek a better life, but they often find that their lives become more difficult. In many cities 25 per cent to 30 per centof the urban population live in poor shanty towns or squatter settlements, or they live on the streets. Of Rio de Janeiro's 10.6 million residents, for example, 4 million live in squatter settlements and shanty towns, some perched precariously on step hillsides. Nevertheless, cities in developing countries continue to attract more and more people.

Table 10.1: Megacities of the World

Cities with 10 Million or More Inhabitants, 1975, 2000 and 2015 (Population in Millions)

City-1975	*Population*	*City-2000*	*Population*	*City-2015*	*Population*
Tokyo	19.8	Tokyo	26.4	Tokyo	26.4
New York	15.9	Mexico City	18.1	Bombay	26.1
Shanghai	11.4	Bombay	18.1	Lagos	23.2
Mexico City	11.2	Sao Paulo	17.8	Dhaka	21.1
Sao Paulo	10.0	Shanghai	17.0	Sao Paulo	20.4
		New York	16.6	Karachi	19.2
		Lagos	13.4	Mexio city	19.2
		Los Angeles	13.1	Shanghai	19.1
		Calcutta	12.9	New York	17.4
		Buenos Aires	12.6	Jakarta	17.3
		Dhaka	12.3	Calcutta	17.3
		Karachi	11.8	Delhi	16.8
		Delhi	11.7	Metro Manila	14.8
		Jakarta	11.0	Los Angeles	14.1
		Osaka	11.0	Buenos Aires	14.1
		Metro Manila	10.9	Cairo	13.8
		Beijing	10.8	Istanbul	12.5
		Rio de Janeiro	10.6	Beijing	12.3
		Cairo	10.6	Rio de Janeiro	11.9
				Osaka	11.0
				Tianjin	10.7
				Hyderabad	10.5
				Bangkok	10.1

Source: UN Population Division, March 2000 (p: 239).

Cities occupy only 2 per cent of the world's land surface, but city populations have a disproportionate impact on the environment. For example, London requires rough 60 times its land area to supply its 9 million residents with food and forest products. Because commerce and trade have spread dramatically in recent years, city residents consume resources not just from surrounding areas, but, increasingly, from around the world. Urban areas also export their wastes and pollutants, affecting environmental and health conditions far from the cities themselves.

What Can be Done?

In the long run, slowing population growth would help ease the pressure on cities, buying time to make improvements in technology. Municipalities also can take a number of steps now—building better transportation systems, promoting recycling and encouraging water conservation.

Public Transportation: One of the best investments that cities can make - both environmental and economic is an efficient mass transportation system. In many cities people waste great amounts of time and fuel going nowhere because traffic congestion is severe. In many urban areas vehicular exhausts account for 50 per cent to 70 per cent of polluting emissions. Curbing the number of motor vehicles by offering transportation alternatives would save energy and reduce pollution. Some cities for example, Amsterdam and Copenhagen—have helped ease the transportation crisis by creating special traffic lanes for bicycles and by urging bicycle use.

Recycling: Recycling mountains of urban waste into new resources makes sense both environmentally and economically. Recycling saves natural resources and reduces the amount of trash deposited in landfills or dumped into rivers, lakes and the ocean. Also, for every million tons of solid waste, about 1,600 recycling jobs could be created in developed and developing countries alike.

Water Conservation: Urbanisation dramatically increases per capita freshwater use, as millions of households gain access to piped water, as industry increases and as large-scale irrigated agriculture replaces subsistence farming. Cities everywhere need to adopt water conservation measures.

11

Cities Residents to the Rescue

In the next ten years, the number of people living in cities will rise to around 3.3 billion. Tokyo already has a population of 27 million, Sao Paulo (Brazil) 16.4 million, and Bombay 15 million. World Bank forecasts show as much as 80 per cent of the developing countries economic growth occurring in the cities and major conurbations.

There are both positive and negative aspects to these developments. At each stage in the history of urbanisation, environmental conditions in cities were improved dramatically. The process was often slow, but over time, many epidemic diseases have been controlled, the supply of clean water and the removal of wastes have become routine, the risks of fire have been contained and standards of comfort and cleanliness have risen to unprecedented levels. Cities could not have become as large and as numerous as they are now if environmental conditions had remained unchanged.

In a curious way, the pollution that cities suffer is largely due to their wealth. The rich consume a great deal more energy, water, building materials and other goods than the poor and thus produce much more waste. This is what is happening, in the cities where rapid industrialisation is taking place—only the rich enjoy the benefits of piped water and refuse collection.

Increasingly Insanitary Conditions

There is another, often tragic aspect to this situation.

The poorest of the poor are reduced to living in outer-edge shantytowns in extremely insanitary conditions and lacking the resources to deal with the problem, the city as a whole has to endure congestion and air and water pollution. Some towns and cities are expanding at a rate of over 7 per cent a year, municipal sanitation departments are no longer able to cope, and it is estimated that as many 30 per cent of the population are without running water.

In many of the world's major cities runaway population growth, an epidemic of Aids and rising social tensions have been combined in the last few years with a steep drop in incomes. The population living on the outer edges of the cities continues to grow apace, hundreds of thousands of people are without running water and 15 per cent of them without sanitation of any sort. Various voluntary bodies and non-governmental organisations have got together, often successfully.

Water and the Environmental Crisis

One key problem concerns the availability of clean water. Some progress has been achieved as a result of the International Drinking Water Supply and Sanitation Decade, but in 1994 at least 220 million people still lacked a source of drinking water near their homes. In some cases, communities of 500 or more inhabitants are served by a single tap. In some towns, communal taps function for only a few hours a day, so that people cannot build up sufficient reserves of water for their personal needs if it takes too long to fetch or if the water has to be carried long distances.

As there are no proper sanitation measures, the disadvantaged members of the population have to drink dirty water, fish in polluted stream and eat vegetables that have been grown by the side of refuse tips.

A further major problem arises from the threefold harmful impact of cities on the environment: urban development on agricultural land, the extraction and exhaustion of natural resources and the dumping of refuse.

Growing pressure on coastal regions, where nearly a billion people now live, is doing serious damage to the marine environment. Development activities pose a threat to nearly half the world's coasts.

Towns originally offered people a place of refuge, of mutual help and culture. According to nineteenth-century town-planning theorists, they should supply all human needs. They were supposed to be the very stuff of civilisation. That was not to be and therefore whenever the authorities throw in their hands, dismayed by the scale of the problems and lacking the political will, money or resources to cope with them, personal initiatives are those most likely to succeed.

12

City Politics

A Voice for the Poor

By 2020 the world's urban population will rise by almost 1.5 billion. Cities and towns house a growing proportion of poor people, partly because of the increased share of urban population of the total but also because economic recession and adjustment policies often hit poorer urban residents the hardest. Cities are associated with economic growth and wealth generation and yet inequality is high. Poor people generally live in substandard conditions, may not benefit from job creation and suffer high levels of pollution, crime and violence.

How can city governments cope with the challenges of population growth and increased global economic competition and meet the needs of poor residents/Is urban governance responsive to the needs of the poor? Are the agencies responsible for city government, especially the municipalities, addressing poor people's needs? Are NGOs and people's organisations playing a greater role in service delivery? Or is their role one of advocacy and lobbying? If so, how do they relate to the formal political system? Can governments fulfil their responsibilities, including poverty reduction? How can the well-being of poor urban governance institutions prioritise their needs? In assessing the responsiveness of city government to poor people, three key questions are addressed:

How Can the Poor Influence the Agenda of the Institutions of Urban Governance?

The influence of poor residents on decision-making is controlled, in part, by the formal political system. Democratisation gives people a vote. However, this vote means more when elected representatives depend on the political support of poor people—where they are a majority, or are well organised, or where there is a ward-based system. If poor people are organised enough, to articulate their needs and demand a fair share of urban resources, NGOs can help poor groups organise better and provide support for networking.

Where poor people are not organised it does not mean they are politically powerless. Poor people in this situation, however, are prey to the disadvantages of patronage and unlikely to be included in formal consultative processes. For an electoral system to be truly responsive, specific mechanisms and channels, such as consultative and participatory processes at city an sub-city levels, are needed to complement representative democracy. Athough, these channels do not necessarily include the poorest or make a marked difference to resource allocation, pro-poor decisions are unlikely without them.

How Can Cities Finance their Activities and Reduce Poverty?

Democratisation has not, in many countries brought allocation of financial resources or the revenue-raising capacity for local governments to fulfil their responsibilities. The responsiveness of city governments to poor people's needs thus depends, on whose voices are heard in the arenas of political decision-making. Responsiveness also depends on how available financial resources are allocated and how the programmes they finance are designed. There is scope, for city governments to increase property and business revenues, and to borrow for capital investment. Whether increased financial resources benefit poor people depends on how the demands of external investors and creditors are reconciled with the demands of poor residents; the willingness of politicians and officials to address the distributive implications of existing and planned spending; and efficient transparent financial management. If funds are made available to sub-city levels of government or if expenditure can be influenced by ward councilors, the funds might then be used to meet the priorities of poor residents.

What are the Necessities of Urban Living and How Can Access to Then Be Ensured?

An Adequate Income: Work opportunities should be the top priority. City governments can, however, support the urban economy in general and the economic activities of the poor in particular. Firstly they can ensure that the basic services are efficiently provided. Secondly city governments can refrain from activities that destroy the assets and livelihoods of the poor, especially eviction of informal settlements and micro-enterprises. Savings and credit schemes can be more appropriately organised at a community level and supported by NGOs.

Land Ownership is a common aspiration for poor households. A home with secure tenure (not necessarily title) provides security, an appreciating asset, access to services and a base for economic activities. Increasing the opportunities for poor households to gain access to a well-located plot of land is an important component of any poverty reduction strategy. Many never fulfil their dream and the needs of those who cannot, or do not wish to become home owners should not be neglected, however.

Local government is potentially more responsive to poor residents than are central government agencies, although this depends on the balance of political power and bureaucratic perceptions. The limited ability of the public sector to secure benefits for the poor from public-private partnerships in land development, suggest that more informal arrangements and the involvement of CSOs may be better ways forward.

Environmental Services: Land alone will not reduce poverty but must be linked to a healthy living environment—a package of appropriate and affordable environmental services, such as public transport, water and sanitation, solid waste collection and energy for cooking and lighting. Rather than discussing appropriate standards, detailed issues of financing and affordability or how continued provision can be assured for each of these services, the research focussed on how far decision making channels, mechanisms and partnership arrangements ensure that providers are responsive to the needs and priorities of poor residents.

Collaborative planning and decision-making arrangements are one promising alternative, despite the current shortcomings of participatory budgeting. For responsiveness to the poor to be built in to such processes, local bureaucrats need to change their attitudes and working practices. Is it possible and acceptable for poor people to have to rely on their own resources, their households and networks—resources that are very limited? Informal networks and links can, however, provide mutual support and access to politicians and bureaucrats, community associations thought not always present, inclusive or transparent, can play an important role in articulating poor residents views and in organising self-help activities. There is scope for formal representative community organisations, for informal links between peoples' organsiations and the power structures and for networking between people's groups. NGOs can play an important role in developing the capacity of community organisations and in facilitating networking. Where NGOs play a role in service delivery. However, there is a danger that the resulting close relationship with local government detracts from their ability to empower poor people and challenge inappropriate policies. City governments, it is clear, cannot cope with the challenges of population and economic growth and respond to the needs of poor people alone. Only in alliance with other actors is there some hope that poverty can be overcome. For CSOs, many of which were forged during struggles for democratisation, this implies moving beyond confrontation to engagement. To form alliances between CSOs and city governments that put the interests of the poor first, poor people must be able to exercise their political rights.

13

For a Broader Approach to Education

In our rapidly changing world, literacy should be seen as an important evolutionary variable in every society. For the further a society progresses, the more it needs to adjust and adapt to new demands and pressures, so that literacy is lifelong necessity for all.

Literacy, in the broad sense, is the foundation for life skills, ranging from basic oral and written communication to the ability to solve scientific and social problems. Today it involves much more than the acquisition of 3 Rs. And a limited set of traditional skills. It is linked with the changing demands of life in a given socio-cultural context.

This means that local communities should be fully involved in defining the content of literacy programmes. The local dimension of literacy is extremely important, not only for accommodating the real needs of learners, but also for taking into account the linguistic and cultural realities of multicultural societies. For in the end, only the learners actually decide what they need to learn.

Building Bridges Between Cultures

Most literacy specialists have accepted this broader, more dynamic and culturally sensitive stance. It marks a long overdue acknowledgement of the positive role that local language and cultures can play in removing some of the serious pedagogical and psychological hurdles often encountered by learners, it is the only way to ensure the relevance and authority of literacy work.

Anyone can insist here on the importance of multilingual education. Today education is as much about learning to live together as learning to know, to do and to be. Yet we cannot live together if our possibilities of expression are limited to a single linguistic frame. This is often at the root of problems encountered in multicultural societies. Of course, inequality in all its forms is a major factor. But internal conflicts often have purely cultural causes. It is more difficult for people to forge links with each other when they cannot communicate linguistically.

Yet children learn languages easily—much more so than the adults who take the decisions. We need to take much greater advantage of this fact. Children are expected to store too much information in their "hard memory"—much of it frankly useless! Giving them language skills provides them with bridges between cultures, enabling them to grow up without the debilitating sense that other cultures are lien. It is our task to try to ensure that education at all levels and particularly basic education, promotes multilinguilism. And we must invest in such education, since to do so is to invest in peace.

It is also important to remind ourselves that literacy is not a neutral process which can be applied in all situations, all the time, regardless of social and economic realities. Such a narrow concept of literacy ignores its critical role as a tool of empowerment. One can treat adult learners as empty vessels waiting to be filled with predetermined bodies of knowledge disconnected from their social experience. Literacy must provide space of intellectual development, motivations for learning and a sense of self-esteem, if it is to be a genuine education for empowerment.

Bringing Adult Education into the Mainstream

Many individuals and families around the world are facing unexpected changes in the pattern of their daily lives, disrupting their plans for the future. The demands on educational services are increasing dramatically, especially in countries where the state is the main provider of education for children and adults. In today's world, we cannot afford a short-sighted approach which, in effect, excludes adult education from the mainstream of the education system, even after the concept of life long learning has been accepted as a framework for educational policy.

Literacy programmes must be given the priority they deserve. Lifelong learning for all requires quality adult education and literacy programmes with qualified personnel, relevant teaching programmes, appropriate post-literacy materials and decent facilities. We must ask ourselves whether we recently are prepared to make the necessary; investments in adult education and literacy to ensure universal access to the types of programmes needed to reach the targets of education for all.

If we truly believe in lifelong learning, and if we seriously believe in redressing the balance of learning in our societies, then we should seek to develop in every country an open and more enabling system of education, breaking with past concepts of education as something which happens to people between the ages of six and twenty and which only the privileged of few were entitled to. Synergy has to be created between formal and non-formal education programmes.

A case in point is the family literacy concept. We all know that the continuing education of parents, particularly when they are illiterate or under-educated, can contribute very effectively to their children's success in school. In fact the family literacy approach is one of the must effective ways of breaking the cycle of inter-generational illiteracy. Education and training policies should include all types of learning, whether it takes place in a school, in the workplace or at home. There should be more innovation and creativity in using methods and approaches.

14

Promotion of Higher Education in Research

The central role of Universities in the development of skills and knowledge as an absolute prerequisite for national development is un-disputed. Higher education institutions have the responsibility for training a country's high level professional, technical and managerial personnel, they are to generate new knowledge through research and advanced scientific training and they serve as agents in the transfer, adaptation and dissemination of knowledge. Higher education institutions also play an important role in contributing to the social cohesiveness of a nation and as a forum for constructive debates on development.

In a world economy which is heavily science-based and technology-driven higher education institutions and particularly universities, have to provide such a competence which is indispensable for building a country's endogenous capacity for problem identification and problem solution through education combined with research. In India, however, universities have so far not been able to fulfil these roles, partly because the multiplicity of their missions is hardly compatible. Many critics of the universities in India consider them to be institutions of learning and research separated from the main stream of the economic and social needs of the population which they are supposed to serve. Most of them have not managed to reconcile the missions of providing country-oriented training and research and of being part of a wider international scientific community. Higher education institutions in many countries all over the world are confronted with a large scale and mostly uncontrolled expansion of the higher education sector and the concomitant growth expenditure against a background of dwindling financial resources to support such expansion. As a result of this expansion the quality of teaching and research has declined due to overcrowding, inadequate staffing, poor physical facilities and equipment. In addition universities often show a poor capacity for management and administration. This results in a low internal efficiency which amongst others is responsible for a rising graduate under or unemployment.

These deficiencies and a lack of national resources produce dependence on external sources particularly for research development. The low capacity for planning and management makes it difficult to properly employ external sources so that there may be pockets of good quality research in one field unrelated to neighbouring areas and not forming part of an endogenous research tradition.

Measures to be Taken

The measures may be aimed specifically at increasing the efficiency of the system of higher education or of individual institutions by improving development relevance, quality and performance. More specifically are:

- to optimise and diversify the structure in line with the country's development requirements;
- to improve the capacity for efficient planning and administration;
- to diversify funding sources, with the aim of relieving the state budget;
- to improve access for talented students from all segments of society, giving special attention to the proportion of women studying.

At the level of individual institutions of higher education the aim should be improve

- education and training performance in the academic-scientific and vocational field;
- research and development capacities, especially in applied fields;
- the capacities to provide consultancy and services to contractors in state, business and industry and society.

In order to achieve these objectives, it is necessary

- to train the academic, administrative and technical staff;
- to improve the infrastructure including central facilities and means of communications; and
- to increase efficiency by improving organisation.

The concept stresses the importance of measures designed to increase the efficiency of higher education in general through the strengthening of management capacities both at the system and at the institutions levels. This extends, inter alia, to the diversification of institutions of higher education in line with development needs, diversification in terms of funding, (including cost-sharing through fees) diversification in terms of study courses and practice-oriented training offered. Academic training at different levels for technical and executive staff.

New Areas of Promotion

The promotion of higher education institutions and subjects considered relevant for development (agriculture, natural sciences, engineering, medicine), the revised concept has to include areas such as the protection of the environment and resources, education, family planning and population policy.

In the wake of the political and economic reorientation taking place in many countries subjects like economics, law and social sciences are increasing in importance.

Prospects

Each country needs capacities which can produce the necessary analytical competence and research for generating information needed for designing and monitoring its development path. Institutions of higher education are essential in providing this competence. The responsibility for advanced education and the production of ideas and information should not be left to external donors. This may entail the concentration of resources, both internal and external, on one or only a few institutions of a country.

15

Population Growth and Education

In contrast to the food supply challenge posed by the coming wave of population growth, the global need for teachers and classrooms will rise very slowly in the next half-century. In many countries, the school-age population is increasing much less rapidly than the overall national population. The trend illustrates that growth rates typically differ for different age strata of the population. It also shows that declining birth rates can take decades to move through an entire population.

At the global level, for example, total population is projected to increase by 54 per cent between 2000 and 2050, but the number of children aged 5 to 14 will grow by only 6 per cent. And of the world's largest countries—accounting for 60 per cent of global population in 1995—will actually begin to see decreases in the number of children aged 5 to 14 by 2015; for several of these countries, the decline in this age group has already begun. These countries will need fewer classrooms and teachers to educate the youngest members of society (assuming they maintain current class size and student-teacher ratios).

Plenty of nations, however, still have increasingly child-age populations. Where countries have not acted to stabilise population, the base of the national population pyramid continues to expand and pressures on the educational system will be severe. In the world's 10 fastest-growing countries, for example, most of which are in Africa and the Middle East, the child-age population will increase in average 93 per cent over the next half-century. Africa as a whole will see its school-age population grow by 75 per cent through 2040.

The rapid growth in African populations is especially worrisome because of the extra burden it imposes in a region already lagging in education. Only 56 per cent of Africans south of the Sahara are literate, compared with 71 per cent for all developing countries. Few African countries have universal primary education, and secondary education reaches only 4-5 per cent of African children. Educating today's children is challenge enough; the addition of another three students for every four already there will require heroic investments in education. But the alternative is grim: without additional investments in education, today's average student-teacher ratio of 42 in Sub-Saharan Africa will reach 75 by 2040.

Many countries will be challenged to increase funding for education while ensuring that other worthy sectors also receive the support they need. With 900 million illiterate adults in the world, the case for a renewed commitment to education is easy to make. But competing for these funds are the 840 million chronically hungry and the 1.2 billion without access to a decent toilet.

The budget stresses on governments attempting to meet these basic needs would clearly be reduced with smaller populations. Mozambique and Lesotho, for example, both met the UNESCO benchmark for investment in education in 1992-6 per cent of gross domestic product—and the two countries economies were roughly equal in size. Yet because Mozambique has many times the population of Lesotho, spending per child in Lesotho is about nine times higher than in Mozambique. For the majority of countries who do not meet the UNESCO funding standard, many of whom also fall short in providing other basic services, a decline in population pressure could help substantially to meet all of their social goals.

If national education systems begin to stress life-long learning for a rapidly changing world, as recommended by a 1998 UNESCO report on education in the twenty-first century, then extensive provision for adult education will be necessary, affecting even those countries with shrinking childage populations. Such a development means that countries that started population stabilisation programmes earliest will be in the best position to educate their entire citizenry.

16

Private Education

The Poor's Best Chance?

Across the developing world, private schools and education companies are not only flourishing, but reaching the poor. India is a case in point. A common assumption about the private sector in education is that it caters only to the elite, and that its promotion only serves to exacerbate inequality. On the contrary recent research points in the opposite direction. If we want to help some of the most disadvantages groups in society, then encouraging deeper private sector involvements is likely to be the best way forward.

Several developments are underway in India, all of which involve the private education sector meeting the needs of the poor in distinct ways. But India is not unique in this respect—similar phenomena are happening all over the developing world.

As a point of departure, how do government schools serve the poor? Usefully, the government sponsored Public Report On Basic Education in India (PROBE) from 1999 paints a very bleak picture of the "malfunctioning" of government schools for the poor. When researchers called unannounced on their random sample of schools, only 53 per cent had any 'teaching activity' going on. In 33 percent, the head teacher was absent. Alarmingly, the team noted that the deterioration of teaching standards was not to do with disempowered teachers, but instead could be ascribed to "plain negligence." They noted "several cases of irresponsible teachers keeping a school closed....for months at a time," many cases of drunk teachers and head teachers who asked children to do domestic chores. Significantly, the low level of teaching activity occurred even in those schools with relative good infrastructure, teaching aids and pupil-teacher ratios.

But is there any alternative to these schools? Surely no one else can do better than government given the resources available? As it happens, the PROBE report were serving the poor and conceded—rather reluctantly—such problems were not found in these schools. In the great majority of private schools—again visited unannounced and at random—there "was feverish classroom activity." Most parents would prefer to send their children to private schools if they could afford them. Private schools, they said, were successful because they were more accountable: "the teachers are accountable to the manager (who can fire them) and through him or her, to the parents (who can withdraw their children)." Such accountability was not present in the government schools, and "this contrast is perceived with crystal clarity by the vast majority of parents".

The Way Forward: Loosen Regulations and Set up Voucher Schemes

To many readers, the existence of these private schools for the poor will come as a surprise. It was to me too, until I had the privilege of conducting field work for the International Finance Corporation (the private finance arm of the World Bank) on a group of such schools operating under the banner of the "Federation of Private Schools" management based in Hyderabad. The federation has 500 private schools (from kindergarten to grade ten) serving poor communities in slums and villages. I was impressed by both the entrepreneurial spirit within these schools—they were run on commercial principles, not dependent on hand-outs from state or philanthropy—but also by the spirit of dedication within the schools for the poor communities served: not for nothing were the leaders of the schools known as "social workers". But these schools suffer under restrictive and inappropriate regulations. One example will suffice: to be recognised a school must deposit upto Rs. 50,000 (about $1.200) in a stipulated bank account, of which neither the capital nor the interest can be touched. Given that the fees charged in these schools ranged from 25 (60 cents) to Rs. 150 per month (about $3.50) with most of the schools grouped near the lower end of the range, such sums are completely prohibitive.

Fees of around $10 per year are not affordable by everyone, but they are to a large number of poor families. Furthermore, the great majority of the schools offer a significant number of free places—up to 20 per cent—for the poorest students, allocated on the basis of claims of need checked informally in the community.

All of this suggests that if one is interested in serving the needs of the poor in India, then trying to reform the totally inadequate, cumbersome and unaccountable government system is unlikely to be the best way. Instead, reform the regulatory environment to make it suitable for the flourishing of private schools for the poor, help build private financing schemes using overseas and indigenous philanthropy and encourage public voucher schemes so that parents can use their allowance of funding where they see the schools are performing well, rather than wasting them in unresponsive state schools.

Private education in developing countries isn't just about the poor, of course and there are many exciting examples of big education businesses. But these too have implications for the ways in which the private sector can reach the least advantaged. One Indian company which embodies much of the excite the National Institute for Information Technology (NIIT). With its competitor, Aptech, it shares just over 70 per cent of the information technology education and training market in India estimated at roughly Rs. 1.1 billion ($24 million). NIIT has 40 wholly owned centres in the metropolitan areas and about 1,000 franchised centres across India. It also has a global reach, with centres in the U.S. Asian Pacific, Europe, Japan, Central Asia and Africa. A key aspect of NIIT's educational philosophy is that there is a need to harness research to improve the efficiency of learning and to raise educational standards.

Because of its success in developing innovative and cost-effective IT education and training, NIIT has attracted the attention of several state governments. First off the mark was Tamil Nadu, which wanted to bring a computer curriculum to all of its high schools. Significantly, although allocating about $22 million over five years to this endeavour, it didn't hand the funds over to government schools, perhaps in light of the PROBE report's lessons. Instead, it developed a model to contract out the service to private companies, which provide the software and hardware, while the government supplies electricity and the class room. For the first round of the Tamil Nadu process, 43 contracts were awarded for 666 schools, with NIIT allotted 371 schools. Many of the classrooms have become NIIT centre, open to school children and teachers I daytime, then used by the franchise holder in the evenings. The contracting out of curriculum areas such as this represents an important step forward in relationships between the public and private sectors and provides an interesting model worth watching and emulating.

Most recently, NIIT has focused on reaching largely illiterate and unschooled children through the Internet. Within weeks of having set up an "Internet kiosk" in a slum area, the institute's researchers found that without any instruction, children could achieve a remarkable level of computer literacy. NIIT is exploring ways to roll out the idea commercially, harnessing the power of the private sector to reach the poorest through modern technology.

These initiatives all find echoes in other developing countries. In each case, the private, not the public sector, is most responsive to the needs of the poor and is brining innovation, efficiency and educational quality to the lives of the most disadvantaged. The private sector has the potential to promote greater equity and to influence education policy, provided it is encouraged and viewed as a partner, not a threat to governments, whether in the developing or the developed world.

17

Will Education Go To Market?

The World Trade Organisation has launched processes that could open up to competition the expanding and highly protected world market in education. What issues are at stake? Mot of us see education as first and foremost a public service which is responsible for providing young people with instruction. For investors looking for somewhere to put their money it is also an annual budget of $1,000 billion worldwide, a sector employing 50 million people and above all a billion potential customers in the form of students.

The decision to extend services the liberalisation of international trade which previously applied to commodities was taken in 1994. The General Agreement on Trade in Services (GATS) which was signed in April of that year included education on the list of services to be liberalised. To say outside the scope of this agreement a country's education system must be completely financed and administered by the state, which is no longer the case anywhere. However, each country can still decide freely what commitments it wants to make and especially which educational sectors it wants to expose to market forces. The New Zealand government, for example, has decided to open up to outside competition the whole private education sector, from primary to university level.

So far, New Zealand is an exception, but that situation is likely to change. Part 4 of the GATS agreement ("Progressive liberalisation") requires that fresh negotiations should be held by the end of 2000 at the latest and should be directed to "the elimination of the adverse effects on trade in services of measures as a means of providing effective market access". At the Geneva headquarters of the World Trade Organisation (WTO), far from the headlines and the demonstrators, work still goes on. But independently of the WTO and national policies, a number of factors are driving educational systems towards "communication".

Pressures for Change

First, education is a rapidly-growing sector in which governments are finding it harder and harder to satisfy demand, above all in higher education. Between 1985 and 1992, the number of students in higher education rose about 26 per cent—from 58.6 to 73.7 million. Meanwhile, public spending on education has tended to stagnate over the past 15 years (5-6 per cent of GDP in rich countries and 4 per cent elsewhere).

In view of this dearth of public spending, parents and students are increasingly looking to private education for a solution. In the United States, every episode of violence in a state school and every scandal that rocks official school systems gives a boost to "home schooling", where children no longer attend school and are taught at home.

Traditional public education is also coming in for strong criticism. Employers complain it is not geared to their needs and is not flexible enough. Under pressure from economic interests, a process of "deregulating" education systems has begun. The growing independence of schools is encouraging them to look for alternative sources of funding, ranging from sponsorship to full management by private companies and including many kinds of partnerships between schools and firms. The time for out-of-school education has come... the liberalisation of the educational process thereby made possible will lead to control by education service providers who are more innovative than the traditional structures.

The development and spread of information and communication technologies on a massive scale make possible the development of paid distance learning, using multimedia and the Internet for tutorials, examinations, etc.

Secondary and primary education are also affected. More and more paying Internet sites bill themselves as alternatives to state schools or traditional private schools. The computer screen takes over from the teacher, for a fee of around $2,250 a year.

The WTO secretariat set up a working group in 1998 to look at prospectus for more liberalised education. Its report pointed to the rapid growth of distance learning and noted the increasing number of partnerships between educational institutions and private firms.

Education for Export

Some 350 U.S. experts on international trade in services, including 170 businessmen and women, gathered at the U.S. Commerce Department in Washington on October 16, 1998 to draw up recommendations for the U.S. negotiators at the WTO. The purpose of the meeting, "called Services 2000, was to look at how the U.S. government should continue to support the efforts of American business to take competitive advantage in foreign markets". The US currently controls about 16 per cent of the world market in services. Its services exports have more than doubled in the past 10 years and now cover 42 per cent of the non-services trade deficit.

The United States is also the world's leading exporter of educational services and a working group at the Services 2000 conference paid special attention to this sector. It concluded that the sector "needs the same degree of transparency, transferability and interchangeability, mutual recognition and freedom from undue regulation or restraints and barriers that the United States acknowledges on behalf of other service industries". The report said that three points should be at the centre of WTO negotiations about education.

Firstly, there should be a free flow of electronic information and means of communication, nationally and internationally. Secondly, the negotiators should tackle "barriers and other restrictions that limit or prevent the provision of educational and training services across countries and internationally." They were also to deal with obstacles to the transferability of degree and diplomas.

Fighting for Market Share

The U.S. demands are backed by most countries of the APEC (Asia-Pacific Economic Cooperation) zone. In a note in October 1999, the Australian delegation to the WTO said it would be "encouraging all members to make expanded commitments in all sectors, even the ones that have proved difficult in both regional and multilateral services negotiations", particularly education.

South Korea took a similar position. At a meeting of Ministers of Human Resources from APEC countries that it hosted in September 1997, the Seoul government put out a memorandum which clearly stated its vision of education as a tool of economic competition.

The emphasis on education for itself or on education for good members of a community without a large emphasis on preparation for future work is no longer appropriate. Such a view of education and work cannot be justified in a world where economic development is emphasised.

"At present, in many economies, the education system do not sufficiently reflect labour market conditions. Their inflexible and inefficient education systems could not meet the new economic environmental challenges." So education should be made more "flexible", i.e. be deregulated and liberalised. In particular, "School systems should be established to allow all students to study what they are interested in and "employers, with school educators, should share the role of educating students".

Some think resistance to liberalising education will come from Europe, especially France. "The future WTO negotiations cannot call in question France's tradition of public service in the field of education and health", stressed a report on the WTO.

18

Shaking the Ivory Tower

Universities have changed radically to keep pace with modern life. Now where are they heading in this high-speed age? In the past half century higher education has been transformed from a privilege conferred on social and political elites to a mass activity available to whole populations. This process began in the United States in the 1940s and 1950s, spread to most of Western Europe and many other developed countries during the 1960s and 1970s and in the past two decades has become a global phenomenon. In the next half century it will accelerate, leading perhaps to the replacement of "higher education" (still an elite-ish category despite its expansion) by extended systems of "lifelong learning".

The key to this transformation has been the expansion of secondary education. For example, in all but two countries of the OECD (Organisation for Economic Cooperation and Development) at least two thirds of young people now complete upper secondary education and so are eligible to enter higher education. The result has been a dramatic increase in enrollment rates in higher education. In Chile the total number of students has grown from 131,000 in 1978 to 235, 000 in 1988 and to 343,000 in the mid 1990s. Even in the United States, the pioneer of mass-assess higher education where very high secondary education completion rates had already been achieved before 1970, the student population has continued to grow, from

11 million in 1978 to 13 million in 1988 and now to more than 14 million.

Two forces have driven up completion rates in upper secondary education and enrollment rates in higher education. The first has been democratisation. As late as 1945 high levels of social and hence educational, inequality persisted even in democratic countries and much of the world remained in the grip of colonial and totalitarian powers. In North America, Western Europe and Australasia democratisation typically took the form of the development of "welfare states", in which there was an increase in public expenditure on education, housing, health and social security that was sustained over more than three decades after the end of the Second World War.

More recently, as renewed emphasis has been placed on the market even in social policy, the rise of consumerism has continued to fuel demands for increased higher education opportunities. The older idea of education as a civil entitlement has been compounded by newer notions of free access to the education marketplace. Far from arresting the advance to mass higher education, consumerism has accelerated it in most developed countries. As traditional forms of social differentiation based on class, gender and ethnic origin have been eroded by democratisation and by market forces, new forms based on educational certification have become more important. In many developed countries the middle class and the "graduate class" have tended to coalesce.

In much of Asia and Africa democratisation took the form of decolonisation. In newly independent countries the energy originally generated in liberation struggles against the colonial powers was directed into a wider struggle to create fairer and more equal successor societies. Education was central to this struggle. The result has been a rapid increase in higher education enrollment—for example, in Tunisia from barely 2,000 students at the time of independence to more than 100,000 today. That process continues.

However, the relationship between democratisation and the development of higher education has been less straightforward in developing countries. Despite very rapid rates of expansion the "metropolitan" influences of the former colonial powers have lingered more stubbornly in higher education than at other levels of education. This is partly due to the continued influence of associations between universities in the British Commonwealth as well as those between francophone universities.

Partly because of these lingering "metropolitan" models and partly because levels of participation are still lower than in developed countries, many African or Asian universities have remained more elite institutions than higher education institutions in North America and Europe. Also, as economic conditions have worsened in some developing countries, the competition between primary and higher education sharpened in the post-independence years as both were seen as equally important priorities. This competition was often reinforced by the intervention of the World Bank.

The second force driving up higher education enrollments has been the changing nature of the labour market. Traditional occupations have become comparatively less significant, while new service occupations, which often require graduate-level skills, have become more important.

Skill requirements have been become more sophisticated. Jobs once done by unskilled or semi-skilled workers are now undertaken by technicians; and those which as recently as the 1980s were taken by technicians are now likely to be filled by graduates. The capital invested for every worker has more than doubled in the past 20 years. Even in occupations where there is less evidence that skills contents have changed significantly, university graduates are now employed in much larger numbers, partly to enhance the social status of these occupations and partly to compete in a graduate-dominated labour market. Healthcare is a good example. Once doctors were the only graduates; today, many para-medical workers are also trained in higher education.

The second form taken by the economic driver has been the growing conviction that national success now depends on economic competitiveness which, in the context of a knowledge-based economy, depends in turn on an adequate supply of human capital. Knowledge is now seen as the key economic resource.

This analysis my be exaggerated; raw materials are still very important in national economies and the global economy. But it has become pervasive—and persuasive. The naïve and linear theories of human capital popular a generation ago which postulated a direct link between investment in education and economic growth may have been challenged; some forms of higher education are now as likely to be labelled consumption as investment goods. Nevertheless, the discourse of the "Knowledge Society" has become even more powerful.

The impact of democratisation and economic competitiveness on higher education has been immense. First, the expansion of student numbers has made the cost of higher education a significant element within national budgets for the first time. A number of important consequences has flowed from this—the opportunity and incentive, to compare the value of investing in different levels of education; increasing demands that universities are run as efficiently as possible (compromising their traditional autonomy from the state—and the market); lower unit costs as budgets have been trimmed (which may have undermined higher education's claim to represent academic excellence). Second, higher education systems have emerged that embrace not only traditional universities but also non-university institutions. Two effects have been produced. One is that the ethos of the traditional university has been eroded; it no longer stands in glorious isolation. The other is that institutional differentiation has been encouraged, whether through active state planning or in response to markets for teaching and research.

The prospects for the next half century are for an acceleration of both drivers—to include access to higher education among the basic entitlements enjoyed by citizens in democratic societies; and to "put knowledge to work" in order to generate wealth and to improve the quality of life. The prospects for higher education during the same period are also relatively easy to predict—increased efficiency (which is likely to include growing pressure to make students contribute more to the cost of their higher education); greater accountability, although more probably in a "market" than a "planning" mode as even the state redefines its role as the purchaser of higher education services, more differentiation, both between and within higher education institutions, as they struggle to identify markets niches; and possibly—growing demands that higher education become more relevant as instrumental considerations triumph over idealistic ones.

However, the future may be more complex than the past. In the second half of the 20th century the encounter between higher education and society has been comparatively straightforward. Although dynamic, society has presented a familiar enough face. It was characterised by a combination of bureaucratic rationality and secular (and liberal) individualism. The beneficence of science and technology was uncontested. The dominant economic model was of large scale industry, or analogous organisations in the corporate and public sectors. Although rapidly evolving, concepts and categories like "career" and "profession" remained valid. Higher education too was familiar enough. Despite the great expansion of student numbers and its adoption of novel roles, the university continued to be recognisable as such. Other types of higher education institution have been deeply influenced by university values and practices.

In the first half of the 21st century both society and higher education may become problematical and so contested categories. Some of these uncertainties are already emerging. Once firm demarcations between public and private domains, whether in terms of the balance between the state and the market or between social "spaces" and individual desires; between producers and users; between investment and consumption; between work and leisure are becoming increasingly fuzzsy in the emerging post-industrials society. Wealth is being generated by the production of "symbolic" as well as—or more than—material goods. Value is created by design, sales, marketing, service rather than by primary production. Institutions of all kinds, civic and corporate, are being challenged by the rise of adaptable and flexible organisations made possible by advances in communications and information technology.

The force of globalisation amounts to much more than round-the clock-round-the world financial markets or an emerging international division of labour; it is not only undermining nation states but also reconfiguring time and space to produce global intimacies, again with the help of the information revolution. Social identities are no longer moulded by the "givens" of religion, class and gender, or by positions within the occupational structure, as they have been since the advent of the industrial revolution in Europe two centuries ago. Instead they are being subsumed by a process of individualisation in which life-styles rather than life-chances predominate.

Higher education will have not only to continue to satisfy the predictable demands for democratic entitlement and socio-economic utility with which it is familiar, but also to cope with the consequences of these new uncertainties. These may include; new curricula that emphasis style and images at the expense of skills and information; recategorisation of higher education as a playful, even selfish activity; a tighter link between experience of higher education and social esteem; submergence of the universal, but also particular, values characteristic of the traditional university by anomic globalisation; threats to the scientific tradition and methods, from the "risk society", from subjectivisation and from demands that other knowledge traditions are accorded equal respect.

The universities of the 21st century, therefore, may have to face two ways. They will have to continue to pay attention to the democratisation and the "knowledge society" agendas, which are likely both to be subsumed in a larger "lifelong learning" agenda. Their ability to sustain current levels of public funding and to satisfy their student-customers will depend on their success in this respect. It will not be easy. There is a danger that the essence of higher education will be lost if it succumbs to unconstrained populism. If this happens, the "quality" of the university will disappear—and with it perhaps its distinctiveness and so its utility and marketability. Similarly in the knowledge Society of the future the university will face new rivals because all organisations will need to become "learning organisations". These rivals strength will be increased if the superiority of universal science is successfully challenged.

But universities will also have to address the new agendas—of the "death" of work (land graduate careers?), of new social movements (and the erosion of individual enlightenments, of globalisation and virtualisation (and the undermining of academic community?); of "alternative" knowledge traditions and perhaps even, anti-cognitive values with the undermining of "objective" science and further erosion of a common intellectual culture.

19

Wiring up the Ivory Towers

Prestigious universities are forging alliances to conquer a share of the e-learning market and stand up to virtual competitors. Just like airline companies, universities around the world are forming partnerships and consortia in response to the pressures of globalisation. The World Education Market held in Vancouver was a timely sign: the fair, expressly organised to foster relations between universities, training providers, software companies and representatives from nations with large education needs attracted participants from over 60 countries.

This race to "partner up" is fuelled by a number of factors. In most industrialised countries, government funding for higher education has decreased, forcing institutions to look for new markets either to subsidise campus programmes or just to remain viable. There is a growing need for lifelong learning as "jobs for life" vanish and the information society drastically reduces the shelf-life of almost any educational qualification. Technological developments, increasingly necessary for learners in all fields to master, offer ever more innovative tools for supporting e-learning.

For business, online learning is "the" new market opportunity with the need for re-training and professional updating predicted to crease an $11.5 billion industry by 2003. Business is better able to develop and maintain the technological infrastructure necessary to run large online systems and everyone, including the universities, recognises that it takes robust telecommunications technology to deliver education and training on the scale demanded.

A host of companies has sprung up to help universities shape and package courses for online presentation, while network providers are jockeying for position to deliver online education.

The United States is the undisputed leader in the field, prompting governments in the U.K., Canada and Australia to commission being eroded by U.S. ventures turned global Canada and the U.K. are in the early stages of setting up their own virtual universities. But what has become clear is that the conservative and labyrinthine decision-making processes which characterise most university procedures are being jolted by a race to get a share of the lifelong learning market.

So far, the most common approach for universities to break into the e-learning universe has been to develop courses specifically for a corporate partner or to form alliances among themselves. Universitas 21, a company incorporated in the U.K. is a network of 18 leading universities in ten countries.

Very often, prestigious universities has stayed clear of going fully online, seeing a danger to their brand name. Many are limiting their offerings to continuing education programmes and/or non-degree courses and more often than not, they are aiming at the corporate market. One company UNext.com, has partnered with first class institutions such as the University of Columbia (U.S.) and the London School of Economics to create online courses marketed under the name Cardean University. Their target: the Fortune 500 companies as well as individual adults. They've managed to attract Noble laureates to design courses and the universities have formed spin-off for—profit companies specifically to develop online programmes. This facilitates the commercialisation of software and other products and is a way to take a commercial approach to continuing and professional studies without compromising the Univesity's standing.

Then there are the free-standing for profit virtual universities which are arousing the ire of institutions that have prided themselves on a long history of public service. The most quoted examplar is Phoenix University, the largest private outfit in the U.S. Now owned by the Apollo Group, it operates the country's largest online programme with 12,200 students. The university tracks students progress and contacts those who don't submit assignments on time or fail to enrol in subsequent courses. Many critics question Phoenix's blatant commercialisation, but few doubt the university's impact on continuing professional development provision.

Although e-learning is in its infancy, its impact can already by gauged. New providers are coming on the market all the time and the trend is accelerating to the point of upsetting universities virtual monopoly in educational accreditation. An Information Technology training course offered or accredited by Microsoft has undoubtedly become more valuable than a Bachelor of Science from a renowned university.

The more consumerist the approach of the education provider, the more what is taught is influenced by demand. MBAs dominate e-learning provision and IT courses are a close second. While the new consumer/learner demands flexibility, choice and just-in-time learning opportunities, suppliers will inevitably arise who are focused on meeting the demand at the expense of quality and value. And is the consumer really the best judge of what course material to choose? Education is a more complex "product" than toothpaste or washing powder. A totally consumer driven education market is unlikely to be in society's best interest in the long term. The commercialisation of education usually goes hand-in-hand with desegregation: course design, delivery, tutoring assessment and accreditation may be carried out by different organisations. Students might study courses or modules from different universities or providers and then put themselves forward for examination and accreditation by yet another institution. While most academics loathe marking assignments, they regard this scenario with horror and blame commercialisation for the demise of the 'community of scholars' concept of a university. The death of the 'course' has also been predicted, with learners—especially corporate and on-the-job learners—demanding short study modules. What then happens to the ability to get an overview of a field when learning consists of the students selecting a whole series of unconnected learning "bites"? Learners will be "zapping" between short sequences or presentations much as they do between television channels.

But while some faculty view e-learning with alarm, technology-based learning is where most of the pedagogical innovation is taking place in universities. Multimedia learning resources and interactive simulations are being developed for the web. Collaborative learning activities, new forms of online assessment and small group teaching technologies are making online courses more stimulating, interactive and attractive than many face-to-face taught courses.

Despite "doom and gloom scenarios", most moderate observers of the scene see a continued future for the campus university, especially at the undergraduate level, while e-learning will above all cater to adult professional and independent learners. Some commercialisation of education is good if it fosters innovation, concern for quality and responsiveness to consumer demands. But if some is good, more is not necessarily better! Not in education at least.

20

Management Training in India

In the developing world as a whole and also in India it can be recognised that a wide "managerial gap" exists between the demand for and supply of indigenous management talent at nearly all levels. This gap constitutes a major constraint in achieving better economic, social and agricultural development.

The importance of developing effective managers is today widely recognised. To achieve economic, social and human development a capable and talented cadre of managers must be developed in each country.

There are several reasons for the paucity of managerial skills in India. Some of these include the rapid expansion of the public sector through the increase in development programmes, the tendency to focus on technical and professional education training rather than administration and management and the inability of so much of the education and training to produce capable managers.

Since Independence India has invested heavily in education and training. Training in management is a complex process. Although the importance of 'good' management to the success of specific development projects as well as to long term national development has been well recognised the nature of 'good' management is culturally specific. Over the past forty years, the development of management skills in India has been mainly treated as a problem of the transfer of techniques. Some Western countries, by virtue of their level of economic development, were supposed to possess know-how about management techniques which could be transferred to other countries lacking this know-how. Future managers and management trainers from less economically advanced countries were sent to school in more developed countries; management experts from these more developed countries acted as consultants and trainers in less developed countries. Such persons taught and learned the only management concepts then known—those developed in the West's more industrialised nations. However, India should develop its own indigenous sources of adaptive managerial theory and practice instead of imitating western concepts.

After the period of formal colonisation an impressive number of management training institutions have been established in India. At the moment, India is not in short supply of management training institutions.

It seems undeniable that management training institutes in India potentially have a huge capability to contribute to the economic development of India.

However a close look at the programmes of India management training institutions and the contribution they give to the development of management reveals that their programmes are mainly focused upon improving the public sector in their regions, while the private sector is left uncatered for.

The public sector is important in stimulating development in India for the coming years the public sector will continue to be the most important employer in India.

Mangers that deal with the public sector need a number of fundamentally different management skills from those that deal with the entrepreneurial sector. Among other qualities, public service mangers must be able to deal effectively with socio-economic policy making and be able to undertake planning and budgeting, they need to know how to get work done by their staff, they need to know how to delegate work. On the other hand, new entrepreneurs need to know how to get started in business, how to write and implement a business plan, how to manage and market a new product development process, how to establish licensing arrangements, and so on.

Management training institutes need to be adjusted to new training and teaching methods developed on the basis of current insights in the roots of the crises in India and mechanisms to overcome these. Some training institutes are making progress in their adjustment process.

Revitalisation of the management training infrastructure in order to establish and restore quality seems to be one of the main elements. If the process of adjustment is taken seriously by the management of the Indian management training institutions, there is certainly a need for some selective expansion of training programmes. If the focus is shifted from training exclusively directed towards the public sector to training likewise for the entrepreneurial sector some expansion is needed.

What is drastically needed is a re-conceptualisation of management training, expanding the concept to include a large variety and multiplicity of learning activities outside of formal classroom training sessions. There are a wide variety of management training approaches and methods available for enhancing managerial talent such as on-the-job training, action training and non-formal training.

There has emerged some widespread agreement during the last years about what might be done to advance concerted action in India to create sustainable development. Management training institutions should contribute to this action.

Development Must be a Human-centered Process

There is widespread recognition now that people at both the ends and the means of development and therefore, that programmes of human-centered development, of food security and of employment must be placed on center-stage of any economic development, strategy, both in the short run and in the long run. Management training institutions should play an important role in human resources development and provide public and private sector officials with skills and knowledge to afford their people with minimum food requirements, to increase the possibilities of basis education and to improve primary health care.

A Strategy of Human Development will not Succeed Unless Production Growth is Restored

The restoration of agricultural and industrial prosperity is necessary both for the achievement of macro-economic objectives—export earnings, import savings, tax revenues, etc. – and of social objectives—employment creation, productivity increases of poor peasants, financial resources for education, health etc.

In this whole era of increasing productivity management training institutions should give public sector officials and private sector employees skills and knowledge about how to increase productivity.

India has these days investment policies to attract foreign investments, however, top executives in both the public and private sectors lack the skills, knowledge and attitudes to implement these policies. These policies could have a major impact upon the environment in India of which the executives might not be aware. These training areas could form a challenge to management training institutions.

India's Development Efforts will Come to Naught Unless Governance is Improved

This clearly raises very sensitive issues. There is widespread agreement now that without improvements in governance, development will prove to be neither equitable nor sustainable. Good governance is based on the observance of certain principles such as accountability of government leaders, transparency in the use of public funds, responsiveness of government to popular aspirations and room for people to participate in all spheres of social and economic life to produce, to organise their mutual assistance, and to express their views on development decisions affecting their existence.

Management training institutions should provide government employees with skills to improve their governance.

21

Wanted:

An New Deal for the Universities

Higher education must meet new demands in order to turn out well-trained professionals instead of unemployed graduate. We are living through a period of profound historical change, marked by an on-going knowledge revolution. Society is changing far more quickly than the structures it has created and the universities are lagging behind these changes. They, and the educational system in general, continue to teach the use of static processes, forecasting models based on historical experience and the memorizing of solutions to already solved problems.

Higher education systems in both North and South are in crisis, both quantitatively and qualitatively. Naturally the developing countries are the hardest hit, both in terms of available resources and levels of student enrollment.

Is the crisis due to a shortage of funds alone? Does the fact that the countries of the North invest ten times more per student than those of the South mean that graduates from the former are ten times better trained? Common sense says yes. But in most cases the answer is no. Generally speaking, university education has failing all over the world, in some cases because it is an offspring of a wasteful society, indifferent to the resources with which that society provides them.

The Missing Link Between Education and the World of Work

In the United States, for example, many teachers and researches come from developing societies which should theoretically have given them a less sound training than that provided by the immense academic and financial resources of the United States system. But this is not the case: they compete professionally and scientifically, with no major problems. In many areas the results of university training are comparable.

Professionals move around because they need jobs and want to work in the best possible working conditions. There are, for example, almost 30,000 African Ph.Ds working in Europe and North America, and thousands of Latin American and Asian professionals working in the Untied States. By the beginning of the 1990s about a million professionals had emigrated to the developed countries over the previous three decades and the figure has increased considerably in the last five years. While the number of opportunities and access to them are uneven, there is little difference between North and South as regards quality; nor is the availability of funding the only basis for improving the system.

The problem is that post-secondary training today is diploma-driven. It is based on rigid study programmes and is changing at a rate which takes little or no account of the speed of knowledge accumulation. This is despite the fact that today's graduate professional needs to have followed a flexible curriculum and must be a problem solver, extremely adaptable to new processes and technologies, generously endowed with creativity and firmly inclined towards lifelong learning, as is clear from the studies on skilled labour done by industrialised countries and from numerous OECD studies.

A recent study of the relationship between higher education and the labour market observes that there appears to be no connexion between the increase in professionals' level of knowledge and changes on the labour market. Although the market undoubtedly demands basic skills and knowledge, it is attaching increasing importance to the emotional and psychological attitudes of future employees.

Although post-secondary education is clearly associated with higher personal incomes, lower unemployment and greater opportunities to climb the social ladder, unemployment rates for people with higher education qualifications continue to be high in both North and South. Graduates unemployment in Europe, for example, varies between 1.4 per cent and 16.6 per cent depending on the country. What's more, many graduates are working in jobs outside their field of training. The increase in graduate unemployment in the developing countries is largely due to the drastic fall in demand from the major employer of graduates-the state—as a result of international competition and new political and economic approaches. The private sector is in no position to absorb the supply of surplus graduates. World Bank studies carried out in Asia, the Middle East, North Africa and certain Latin American countries show that graduate employment is increasing.

All the same, higher education cannot be held wholly responsible for graduate unemployment nor for the correlation that should exist between training, study programmes and demand for labour. It is often said that higher education is failing to provide training in the activities required by the market, but the market is often incapable of adequately anticipating the type of professionals it is going to need.

A survey conducted in Florida (USA) among multinationals in the high-tech and services sectors reveled companies that were unable to identify the professional qualities that would be required within ten years and, in many cases, within five years. This is not surprising, in view of the spectacular rise of the Internet between 1994 and 1998 which caught many hardware and software firms unawares. It is in information technology that redundancies and high unemployment levels are occurring, because systems are constantly changing and because of strategic mergers between the major companies.

Another example of the difficulty of making reliable predictions concerns those made by the European Community and the US Government regarding the type of jobs that would be needed at the beginning of the new century. These predictions were inaccurate: what had been forecast to occur after 2001 actually came about in the late 1980s and early 1990s.

It can be said, however, that professional training over the come years will focus on areas such as high-tech electronics, information technology, aqua-culture, agro-energy, biotechnology and energy physics. Jobs in information and communication systems will require new qualifications which will have to be continually updated. The service sector will experience spectacular growth in the field of leisure and recreation because of the reduction in working hours. New professions in the human sciences such as "ludicadology", incorporating psychology, pedagogy, information science and the technology of education, play and creativity programmes, will replace the old single-discipline approach.

In short, the great occupational change looming ahead will call for increased interdisciplinary, revitalisation of the disciplines related to thick and aesthetics and sweeping changes in the attitudes of teachers and students: for the professional of the future, education will be a lifelong process and education and work will go hand in hand.

The great challenge will thus be to create a stable relationship between higher education and society through strategic alliances with the production system designed to promote participation by all sectors of the economy in the university's basic and applied research programmes and by production-sector specialists in university teaching.

The problems of the university are also those of society, and so are the responsibilities. This rises the question of the university's specific culture, especially the teacher-student relationship. Planning is currently based above all on the teaching staff, which is more corporatist than academic. Physical spaces, salary scales, curricula, structures and timetables are more closely geared to the needs of the teacher than of teaching. This is the case all over the world.

More serious still, this teacher-centred culture is giving way to one that is even more dangerous for the survival of university education: an administration-centred culture. This would mean an education system dominated by bureaucrats and the kind of management structures which would place an institution whose function is to produce and disseminate knowledge on the same footing as a detergent factory or a multinational travel agency.

But no strategy for change can work unless higher education adapts to the challenge of the knowledge explosion. It is vital that course content should be geared to what learners "must know" and not to what teachers "know" or "think they know". This will force teachers into a permanent renal of theories, techniques and processes, keeping up with knowledge produced both inside and outside the university. Higher education is evolving towards a model in which lecturers and students will be permanent learners and where curricula will be drawn up on the basis of innovation, fresh knowledge and the latest teaching and learning technologies. Above all the university must teach people to think to use common sense and to give free rein to the creative imagination.

22

Corporate Ambitions in Education

Centralisation and efficiency, frequently invoking the powerful metaphor of scientific management or "Taylorism," using the stopwatch and management to discover the "one best way." These principles had been instrumental, industrialists of the time believed, in creating the industrial revolution and the wealth of powerful international companies. The quest for efficiency of those decades led to the problems we must now repair, notably the rigid and bureaucratic structure of our school systems.

Today, public schools continue to adapt new business efficiency techniques in what seems to be a constant recycling process. Scientific management, it turns out, was only the precursor to a host of ever newer management theories aimed at encouraging greater worker productivity and hence greater national wealth.

When Schools Become Levers to Attract Business Investment

These trends have echoes in the management reforms prescribed for and adopted by schools. Some seek increased efficiency through decentralised school governance while others imagine that outsourcing (or contracting) the management and operation of schools will lift educators' performance because incentives are lacking to secure government jobs.

All this is happening against the backdrop of economic globalisation, which inevitably creates political tensions by pitting governments against one another in competition for transnational corporate jobs and global capital. Our current era mimics the turn of the century to the extent that international capital flows and transnational production processes influence both corporation and governments. Today, technologically induced speed, growth among investors, concentration of wealth, and interconnectedness have increased the effects of this global speculation and decreased the capacity of governments to regulate business and markets. Not surprisingly, this global market ideology has been broadly recognised as a force in national education policy.

Reforming local schools becomes one of the ways that cities engage in the global competition to provide production resources to corporations. When formal schooling is seen as a key element of productive capacity, a view reinforced by the decline of manufacturing and the rise of information-based technologies, the quality of the local public school system takes on renewed importance for business leaders and local politicians alike. Today's corporate leaders have uncommon access to elect political officials and government agency heads, the wealth of large corporations to draw upon and the ability to affect local and regional economics simply by making business decisions.

Schools are treated as engines of economic development to lure business to a particular city or state, so corporate and local political leaders cooporate in their governance and redesign. In short, school policy becomes labour policy?

This powerful combination of corporate, national and state executives is happening at the expenses of education professionals. In contrast to the turn of the century, when educators played a pivotal role in debates by emphasising the role of schools in developing citizenship, today they have been largely discredited. Selecting school leaders from outside the field has become both symptom and spur to this decrease in the educator's status. A small but influential group of school districts is choosing leaders from among the ranks of businessmen, politicians and the military, rather than educators.

All this is taking place with little evidence that recent management solutions will turn around poor schools, nor that improvements in school performance protect against declines in productivity or the business cycle. Yet there are more troubling problems with reform strategies that pit the market against government in education. One is that education is reduced to its narrowest economic purposes. According to a 1992 survey, corporate executives most want schools to emphasize "a basic understanding of math and science:" and "sound work habits such as self-discipline, timeliness and dedication to work." These are laudable goals, but reflect a narrow set of traits that employers predict their workers will needed in an information economy their workers will need in an information economy.

The corporate model of reform pays little heed to other expectations of public schools: building just and tolerant communities, reducing distrust of one another and our shared institutions, safeguarding democratic ethics and introducing children to the cultural wisdom of the world. We are also witnessing the abandonment of many kinds of equality. Neither markets nor business ethics routinely put equality or fairness above profits. Whole groups of people will not fit the prevailing model of what it takes to be competitive in an educational market place in which competition is the guiding principle of improvement. Another disturbing trend is the anaemic citizenship that economic justifications for schooling envision. Increasing the emphasis on individualism is likely to exacerbate a pattern of civic disengagement many already find disturbing in its scale and scope.

A Balancing Act to Reach a Healthy Equilibrium

We need a contemporary counter-movement to restore a healthy equilibrium of goals for our public schools. This movement would be grounded in a very different educational critique that rejects the metaphor of market (or management) failure and instead tackles the problems in our schools as symptoms of a widespread civic breakdown. The solutions to school failure would then hinge on common concerns, rather than rigorous individual competition and accountability. In addition to academic criteria, parents and reformers would craft student performance measures that reward active citizenship, tolerant and respectful behaviour and cultural knowledge in the arts, history and languages. This reform movement, seeking equity and tolerance, would revitalise democratic institutions and not merely aim for more efficient production.

23

Violence in Schools

A World Wide Affair

In all countries, schools are magnets for strife in society. Dealing with these tensions calls for extreme caution, for fear of making matters worse. Violence in schools is a world wide problem: it exists in rich and poor countries alike. It's chiefly a male phenomenon, hitting a peak when boys turn 16 years old in some countries and 13 in others. Experts agree at least on one point: this violence cannot be pinned to a single cause. Instead, they point to complex patterns linked to family situations. Socio-economic conditions and teaching methods.

Tackling Segregation

But these are just indicators and do not justify any deterministic explanations. When researchers say that 10 to 20 per cent of risk factors are linked to single parent families, this suggests that 80 to 90 per cent of such families are not the source of any violence. A child form a slum area with a teenage mother or a father in jail will not automatically be violent! Likewise, experts say there is a "hard core" of violent children—about five per cent of the total. One can found that this figure can vary between one and 11 per cent. The school itself can be an aggravating factor, through high staff turnover or "ghetto classes" to which poorly-performing students are relegated. These "hard core" groups, then, cannot be deemed "inalterable". On the contrary, something can be done about them.

Should they simply be expelled, as some advocate? Such a measure would only make their segregation and sense of exclusion worse. And they are, after all, at the root of the whole problem. The solution lies partly in developing customised projects, but most importantly, in strengthening economic social participation.

To put an end to school violence, we need a well-established state with the means to compensate for inequalities, a state that tries to re-establish diversity in neighbourhoods and schools, one that does not give up on the notion of justice for children, as some are demanding.

Passing the Torch

We should also try to lift schools out of their fortresses, so they do not become the symbol of a society that excludes people. Projects in the Netherlands, Brazil and the United States have shown that schools can be vibrant places that provide social, medical and cultural services to a neighbourhood.

In the Brazilian state of Minas Gerais, for example, there is a vocational school where elderly craftsmen teach their skills to teenagers. Such contact between generations can offer a very valuable social education. "It takes a village to educate a child", goes an effort an African proverb. Let's make an effort to seek out these opportunities, even in the most heartless cities.

24

Beyond Economics

Unless policymakers take a more all-round view of education, they risk sending their countries down the wrong path. Over the past decade, educational change in most countries has been driven by one imperative: survival in the global economy. This process has been particularly salient in the Asia-Pacific region following the drastic shock of the 1997 economic downturn. But in the current reform process marked by speeding commercialisation and economic preoccupations, other educational missions are being ignored, and countries risk paying a high price for their short-sightedness.

There's no denying that economic considerations are critical in today's world. Students have to acquire the knowledge and skills to survive and compete in the global economy, especially one which more than ever before prizes human capital. A high-quality labour force gives nations a cutting edge in global competition. Understandably, stressing economic returns in the current educational debate attracts private resources. But education has other functions that are the indispensable corollary of more balanced, equitable development. They deserve to be briefly explained.

The first is a social function: education has a role to play in facilitating social mobility and bringing about integration in often very diverse constituencies. It is at school that children learn how to form a broader set of relationships, to live together and become aware of belonging to teach us civic attitudes, to make us aware of our rights and responsibilities—in essence, to become responsible citizens. The task is fundamental in light of democracy's advance in so many countries over the past decade or so. Then there is education's cultural function. Developing creativity and aesthetic awareness, accepting other traditions and belief systems while valuing our own are all part of the path towards fulfilment. Finally, education is a goal in and of itself. Schools help children learn how to learn and play a pivotal role in transferring knowledge from one generation to the next. I believe that all these facets of learning are critical for the long-term prosperity of our societies. In our globalised, interdependent world, these functions take on a more international character. Everywhere, education has a role to play in eliminating racial and gender biases, promoting global common interests, moments for peace and greater international understanding.

Rising Above Short-term Pressures to Strike a Harmonious Balance

While education is widely recognised as the spine of the learning society, the complexity lies in striking a balance between these various functions. The commercialisation of education that we are witnessing the world over inevitably pushes schools, educators, parents and policymakers to pursue short-term, market-driven outcomes. Lawyers, bankers and businessmen have an increasingly high profile in educational debates. Following Southeast Asia's downturn in 1997, they were influential in changing the academic mindset. In little time, emphasis has shifted from academic achievement to developing communication skills, creativity, adaptability. In and of itself this is not necessarily regrettable. The problem is that these skills are all perceived to be at the service of a supreme economic value.

Sounder research will be required to analyse and assess where the current trends are leading us. It is increasingly recognised, however, that unless economic growth is accompanied by good governance, a fair sharing of benefits, better social and environmental protection and attention to culture, it will, sooner or later, lead to unrest. It is through education that this broad spectrum of concerns can be nurtured. Policymakers who have taken stock of this holistic mission unfortunately represent a minority in today's educational debates and reforms. Their foremost challenge is to manage commercialisation, to rise above short-term pressures and to take a more ethical stance towards education, a long-term strategic view.

25

Technological Entrepreneurship

The New Force for Economic Growth

Entrepreneurship has emerged as a major new force for change. The dynamic role of modern small business in economic growth has received fresh recognition worldwide. It is essential to promote entrepreneurship and to mobilize the dynamism of the private sector for accelerated national development. An unbridled private sector may not, however, ensure growth with equity. It is the prime responsibility of governments to create policy frameworks that enable businesses to apply technology for competitive advantage and for the well-being of the public.

The Changing Global Environment

As agents of change and progress, entrepreneurs start by identifying a market opportunity and matching this with social or technical innovations. They then proceed to mobilize the resources necessary to drive their business concept to its commercial realisation. The development of a product or service with a high technology content—never easy anywhere, or at today's rapidly changing global environment. It calls for restructuring the available technology and business development systems and developing the skills needed by a new breed of "techno-entrepreneurs" to transform innovations into market opportunities at home and abroad. It also requires reorienting the present processes and priorities of technical and economic cooperation among countries.

Amidst the global concerns of environmental preservation, poverty elimination and social development, the practical problems of entrepreneurship are not being properly addressed, even though entrepreneurs will create the bulk of enterprises, jobs and wealth.

A torrent of technology-based goods hits the market every week, ostensibly improving the quality of our lives while simultaneously creating complexity and dislocation. The pace of progress in information technologies, microelectronics, robotics, new materials, biomedical sciences, space science and other advanced technologies quickens, significantly changing the way we live. The growth of markets for these technologies also proceeds apace.

Further, technological change is taking place today against a background of growing intra-national and international disequilibria. While the transformation from State-centred to market-oriented development is opening up enormous opportunities and options, it has also caused severe short-term hardships. In order to survive and prosper in these changing times, India and its enterprises need enlightened government policies, good technical infrastructure and strong cultural roots.

Traditional production factors are giving way to a new paradigm characterised by new patterns of trade, investment and employment, and by informal networking life-long learning and technological entrepreneurship. The manufacturing sector in India continues to be dominated by food products, textiles, chemicals and other traditional industry, mainly in the public sector. However, change is coming, albeit slowly. State enterprises are being corporatized pending privatisation and the share of knowledge-based and information-related activities in the marketplace is rising perceptibly. Restructuring policies now place emphasis (often purely rhetorical) on the role of the private sector. The legacy of decades of centrally-planned development is generally inimical to private enterprise. In turn, the private sector has been slow to respond to economic liberalisation in India and generally failed to generate the new employment necessary to absorb new entrants to the labour force.

The regulatory problems of an onerous tax structure and administration, poor access to finance and raw materials, over-regulation of labour and land use, pervasive bureaucracy and restricted markets have been significant barriers to entrepreneurial growth.

Towards Competitive Performance

The imperative of improved performance has serious implications for India if it is to survive, stay abreast and succeed. It calls for national efforts on systemic efficiency and productivity growth, the move from an investment-driven to an innovation-driven economy and sustained higher-order competitiveness; towards enhanced customer satisfaction at home and penetration of selected markets abroad. Concurrently, governments and business have to address such intractable problems as poverty, corruption and the degradation of the environment.

Creating New Technology-based Ventures

Starting a new business in India is a hazardous task. Problems are compounded when the venture is technology-based:

- Capital requirements are generally larger, while traditional banks are ill-equipped to process the perceived risk. Venture capital generally only becomes as option when the venture has documented the merits of its management, market and innovation.
- Knowledge-based ventures can benefit form linkages to sources of knowledge—e.g. the technical university or research lab. Such mentoring needs to be cultivated.
- Techno-entrepreneurs often have technical skills but usually lack the business management and marketing skills necessary for success. These need to be supplemented.

- In fields where technology is changing rapidly, it is often advantageous to make technology-acquisition arrangements. Souring such innovations, negotiating technology licensing agreements and protecting the intellectual property itself require special skills.
- Knowledge-based innovations are inherently more risky than others. The management of this unique risk requires assessment techniques and vision.
- Technology-based ventures often have social and environmental implications, which need to be managed carefully.
- Penetrating a competitive market requires good market intelligence, a good strategic plan and good luck.

Special Characteristics of "Techno-entrepreneurs"

The popular misconceptions are that techno-entrepreneurs are born, not made; that they take risks with other people's money and fail more often than they succeeded. In fact, entrepreneur skills can be identified and developed. The entrepreneur is typically an innovator who formulates new solutions to existing problems, mobilises resources and stimulates others to participate in his or her team. These aptitudes develop over time, often starting in childhood, as the person faces new challenges and learns from failure.

Entrepreneurial opportunities can be found in every industrializing country, community and family. Principal sources of entrepreneurs for knowledge-based ventures are often the university and government research laboratories, the large industrial and military establishments and professional service firms. Some motivations of the entrepreneur are the need to: be independent; create value; contribute to society; earn recognition; become rich or; quite often, simply not to be unemployed. Value-adding ventures with good growth potential can best be developed in an open market and in a culture, which supports risk-taking.

The techno-entrepreneur anywhere has the challenge of moving a concept through the prototype and production phases towards creation of a product which meets market needs at a price consistent with the value created and with the ability of customers to pay.

Equally important, the market itself has to be developed and sustained. It is not enough to be first with a better mousetrap if one does not have the skills to educate and reach potential buyers and to set the market standard.

Hence one has to distinguish between innovators and inventors. The inventor is typically a creative person in a quest for knowledge or for producing new products, without determining in advance whether a real market exists for his or her inventions. On the other hand, the innovator draws on existing knowledge and the talents of others to develop or adapt a product or service at a volume and cost that can capture a significant portion of an identified market. The flexibility and creativity of a small entrepreneurial techno-venture may lead to more incremental and break-through innovations than can be generated by larger-sized firms in many sectors.

The pace and pattern of India's economic development now depend in large measure on its technical resource base. In this context, the key determinants are the skills to apply technology for enhanced competitiveness, as well as to create techbased ventures. Techno-entrepreneurs have to be supported by appropriate national structures and international linkages if they are to survive and flourish in an intensely competitive world.

26

Employment and Poverty Alleviation

Today the key socio-economic problem is large scale unemployment. Spreading joblessness brings many other problems in its wake. It erodes national incomes and living standards, aggravating the already grindingly difficult job of promoting development and alleviating poverty. Joblessness also raises government budget deficits, increasing macro-economic instability while soaking up investment for productive capital expenditure, education, training and relief aid. And joblessness ruins lives and communities by depriving people of the dignity and satisfaction that comes with earning one's keep and making a contribution to the well-being of family and society.

Theories about how best to nurture development (and thus create jobs) have shifted considerably over the last decade. The state role has evolved, in the minds of many, from being a source of relief for the problems of unemployment, poverty and underdevelopment, to being a fundamental cause of these problems through the distorting impact of its intervention on the market.

However, the more market-oriented philosophy that grew up during the 1990s has yet to provide convincing solutions in practice at least not on a grand scale and especially not in terms of job creation as the present jobless economic recovery demonstrates.

The weakness of the current recovery and past approaches to economic development can be traced to the failure to consider employment as the predominant means of promoting growth and alleviating poverty. In policy circles it has too long been an almost ignored priority.

Current trends thus bode poorly, particularly as unemployment rates soar. In light of the circumstances, we need to begin re-examining some of the fundamental questions—if only to find out what has gone wrong with the answers.

Minimum Wage?

Let's begin with wages. With corporate restructuring in full force on a global scale, are low wage rates required to raise employment and maximize profits? A top manager of a multinational consumer electronics group certainly thinks so; he likened the perfect factory to a ship "so that we could move it around the world to where labour was cheapest". Perhaps, but this bottom-line emphasis on unit labour costs ignores at least two other factors; namely, that higher wages can act as a screen to select more productive workers and that higher wages translate into better productivity via improved worker nutrition, increased consumption and a generally healthier quality of life.

If higher wages bring these benefits (and it is an open question) should government insist that there be a minimum wage rate? Neo-classical economists tend to respond "no", assuming that a higher wage rate puts money into the pockets of some low wage workers while forcing many others out of work because companies cannot afford to pay them.

Technology Transfer

The impact of technology is another area in need of study. Technological innovation is usually labour-saving and tends to originate in industrialised countries, moving towards developing countries like India, Pakistan where labour tends to be low cost and abundant. Would it therefore make sense to slow down or somehow restrict technology transfer, especially to development markets, in the interest of preserving employment?

The answer here is clearly—No. Historical evidence abundantly demonstrates that attempts to retard technological progress bring about greater poverty and lower growth. Technology, infact, is at the heart of the new endogenous growth theory which is very much in vogue among development economists today. Slowing down or inhibiting technology transfer would certainly dash many countries' development hopes and aggravate poverty. However, the relationship between technology, development, employment and poverty alleviation is not without its complications.

In the 1980s, the buzz word among development specialists was "appropriate technology", i.e., small-scale and labour-intensive technologies that would increase productive output while allowing an equilibrium solution to be found such that the ratio of the productivity of labour to that of capital is proportional to their relative prices. The conditions for this "small is beautiful" approach to technology tended to be best met in agricultural production. However, where manufacturing industry is concerned, the small-is-beautiful approach foundered badly when the only viable technological alternatives proved to be highly capital-intensive.

Development Gap

A wide gap has emerged between developing countries with an inward focus (which tended to be protectionist and pursue policies of import substitution) and those with an outward focus and a policy of pursuing export-led growth. Competing in international markets requires technology that is as good as or better than that found in advanced, industrialized nations. Small, therefore, is not beautiful in the global manufacturing economy where product standards are high and the elasticity of substitution between labour and capital is very limited.

The drive to obtain state-of-the-art technology thus leads to a policy conundrum: it is a pre-condition for success in manufactured exports, but the impulse to compete successfully in this most lucrative sector speeds up the transfer of technology from the developed to the developing world, thus reinforcing the bias toward labour saving equipment in developing countries and accelerating a process that is seen as a source of job loss in the industrialised countries.

Technology and Jobs

Before concluding that modern technology transfer is inimical to employment in developing countries, we have to distinguish clearly between technology's static and dynamic consequences. In a static sense, it is true that highly capital-intensive export industries may not create much employment on a net basis, but the dynamic effects of technology transfer do contribute to economic growth. And growth, in turn, generates multiplier effects in the form of demand, which stimulates ancillary production activities (like food processing or consumer goods) that rely on more labour-intensive technologies.

The problem is that the diffusion and application of technology on a global scale blurs the categories of international product specialisation and creates a much more competitive and conflict-prone international environment.

For example, we have already seen the Asian Tigers move from producing goods such as textiles and processed food to producing hi-tech and value-added consumer durables. This advance is only possible due to the growth of human capital (facilitated by investment and higher incomes) and it leaves production of textiles to other industrialising countries, like Indonesia, the Philippines and now China. But the dynamic comes at the expense of jobs in industrialised regions, like the US and the EC, which lost more than a quarter of their work force in textiles during the 1980s. In spite of job losses, advanced countries continue to produce textiles, notwithstanding major differences in the hourly wage rates for spinning and weaving and the fact that essentially the same hi-tech equipment is being used in most production centres.

Protectionism

What has happened in textiles is happening in other industrial sectors (automobiles, for example) as well. The intense market competition is proving to be a source of trade conflicts and possibly protectionism, as jobs come under increasing pressure.

For many workers and managers, the benefits of foreign direct investment look increasingly like a zero-sum game for employment and there is a real risk that the tenuous link between overall growth and employment will break down altogether. It is hardly surprising that we are already seeing negatively affected workers and local businesses clamouring for protection in advanced countries.

Governments Role

The concerned governments are suppose to carry out much of this research. The three initial lines of inquiry follow from three reasonable assumptions about the future.

- First, increase in welfare and consumption subsidies are out; investments in training and human capital are in. How can investments in human capital be directed to positive employment effects? Is it perhaps not time to explore more fully benefit schemes targeting the unemployed and the unskilled poor providing them with the type of subsidies that would enhance their human capital, improve their health and productivity through better nutrition and preventive medicine and restore the dignity of holding a job?
- Second, given the quasi-inevitability of increased automation in manufacturing, how can other sectors (particularly agriculture and services) be developed to

export their long-term potential for employment creation?

- Third, given the inevitable pressures of work and productivity in the global economy, what sort of alternative institutional arrangements need to evolve with respect to industrial relations, employment and work conditions?

Finding answers to these and other questions will require no small amount of new thinking, but parochialism or a failure of imagination would be fatal flaws in this global era.

27

Water

An Educational and Informative Approach

The most characteristic element of our planet is undoubtedly water. Indeed, more than two-thirds of the earth's surface is covered by water—the total volume representing almost 1,500 million cubic kilometers. About 94 per cent of this water is found in the oceans, almost 6 per cent is located underground and in glaciers whereas rivers, lakes, soil moisture and atmospheric vapour, which constitute the major source of drinking water, account for a mere 0.0221 per cent of the total volume.

Water is indispensable for all living organisms. Life, as we know it, is impossible without water. It is present in all aspects of our life—directly or indirectly next to the air we breathe and together with the soil that we live upon, water constitutes the most important part of our environment, our most precious resource. And yet, except in the arid or semi-arid regions of the world, its value is generally overlooked until some catastrophe—natural or man-induced—forces our attention to its worth. But even so, no sooner is the situation remedied than, more often that not, we revert to our old attitude.

The reason for this sort of indifference is undoubtedly attributable to the fact that, except in exceptional circumstances, water has always been considered as a "gift of the gods", as some thing that human beings are as naturally entitled to as the air they breathe. Its supply, however uneven, has always seemed inexhaustible because water has a natural regenerative cycle which, until the present century, was beyond human control or interference-or even proper comprehension. But the trend of social, political and economic evolution, notably in the past 200 years, with an increase of industry, agriculture, technology and above all, a vertiginous population growth, as led to a dramatic revision of the age-old belief that no demands made by human populations on the natural resources of the planet are in the process of setting in motion vicious circles in the environment from which it is becoming increasingly difficult to extricate ourselves, not only as concerns the present, but far more important, for the future. Thus, the overuse—or abuse—of water resources has started affecting seriously not only the water cycle but the very nature of water in such a way that, in conjunction with other abuses of the environment, the results have been climate changes, droughts, flooding, desertification on the one hand and acid rain, water pollution and eutrophication on the other.

Actually, the problem of water is to be considered less in terms of quantity—though with a steeply increasing world population making increasingly heavier demands on a fixed quantity of water, one will sooner or later be confronted with this aspect of the problem too—than in terms of proper distribution of available resources taking into account sound management, stock-age and maintenance of quality. For among the major preoccupations of humanity in the coming years, adequate supply of freshwater to the teeming populations figures in the forefront. Between 1900 and 2000 water consumption will have globally increased tenfold and though the share of agriculture, the major consumer of fresh water, is expected to drop significantly (from 90 per cent to 62 per cent approximately), that of industry and the cities will have increased enormously (approximately, from 6 per cent to 24 per cent and 3 per cent to 8 per cent respectively).

Given the current trend of societal evolution i.e. greater emphasis on industry and increasing migration towards the cities added to the global population boom, these figures are certainly cause for concern. Not only because of the damages caused to freshwater resources through the increasing use of fertilizers in the search to maximize agricultural production to cater to the increasing populations, but equally because the mushrooming of industries and urban concentrations are sources of increasing water pollution. Though the industrialised nations have more than their fair share of blame in this matter insofar as the current state of water pollution goes, for the future, it is in the developing world that lies the major source of concern. Lack of resources for adequate urban planning, the increasing role of industry in the search for economic solutions added to uncontrollable population pressures are already on the way to creating an explosive situation in a great number of developing nations with the available water supply becoming more and more inadequate in terms of quantity as well as quality. And when one considers the fact that around 80 per cent of all diseases are estimated to be water related and that by the year 2000, 51 per cent of the world population will be urban based, one can hardly be accused of exaggeration in speaking of an explosive situation.

Attacking such a vast problem is no mean task. Water being at the very source of life, what concerns water concerns every aspect of life. Thus, be it climate change, pollution, desertification, deforestation, food production....or whatever other major environmental problem that humanity is confronted with today, water constitutes one of the prime factors. Managing our water resources with care and intelligence for the use of present and future generations is a major responsibility which has to be shared by governments and the public alike, for no sector alone can deal efficiently with so vital a problem which affects not only the present but also the future of humanity. Again, as in the case of biodiversity and climate change, the problem of water being a global problem, international cooperation is of utmost importance since activities in one part of the planet are likely to produce consequences in other regions of the world. Concerted action by the international community alone is capable of dealing effectively with a problem of such far-reaching consequences.

If our planet is to be saved from disaster—for in jeopardizing our water resources we are guilty of nothing less than condemning life itself on our planet—we have to work for sustainable results: short-term plans for the present which will dovetail into medium-term ones for the coming generations without compromising the possibility, at the same time, of careful long-term planning to guarantee the future of the planet. In this, the part of environmental education and information of the people is fundamental. No strategy, no policy, no plan—be it ever so well prepared and implemented—can hope to succeed without the active and effective participation of the main actors—the people who must be properly educated and informed. For this age-old techniques, beliefs-mentalities must be brought in line with present day realities. People have to learn to think differently in order to veer from a course which, however right in the past, has been shown to be less than adequate for present conditions—and catastrophic for the future—and must therefore needs be altered.

Changing mentalities is neither an easy nor a rapid process. It is difficult to go back upon the accumulated experience of generations—even in the face of stark realities and scientific evidence. Moreover, when dealing with such global and fundamental issues as water, where even "scientific evidence" tends to be stated in tentative terms, the task becomes more onerous. Add to this the fact that the problem presents itself most presently in developing countries which are equally subject to enormous economic pressures which tend to reduce the cope of possible solutions. We are thus faced with the enormous task of trying to change attitudes, values, mentalities of populations whose geographical, socio-cultural and economic conditions have already fashioned priorities other than those that would precisely permit them to overcome their difficulties in a sustainable manner. In other words, of persuading people to abandon traditional short-term strategies in favour of perhaps more unattractive but eventually sustainable, long-term practices.

A veritable Herculean labour—which can only be accomplished through information and education. And in particular, through environmental education and information whose avowed aim is precisely to develop the understanding, knowledge, skills and motivations leading to the acquisition of attitudes, values and mentalities which are necessary to deal effectively with environmental issues and problems. Sound and systematic environmental education of the people associated with concerted local, national and international action, is the only means to finding a sustainable solution to this problem. The ground has to be paved through adequate information on the subject followed by educative processes adapted to specific local conditions. For a uniform education, whether formal or non-formal, might perhaps do more harm than good as its rejection, due to its unsuitability in the light of local customs, beliefs, traditions.., might only serve to reinforce the very attitudes that it seeks to change. In each region, each country, each locality the educative processes must correspond to the socio-cultural, historical, economic conditions of the people. Only then can we hope to arrive at the change in mentalities around the planet which, coupled with consistent, parallel support from national and international institutions, will lead to the safeguard of what is perhaps our most precious resource—Water.

28

Resistance to Change

Why Poverty Reduction Programmes did not Work

Poverty reduction as an overall objective of the global development industry is not new. The only problem is that so far it has not really worked. Despite several decades of economic growth and huge development aid disbursements, the number of countries the United Nations calls "least developed" (those with a per capita income of less than US$ 900 a year) has in fact nearly doubled since 1971, from 25 to 49. In the last decade (1990-2000) and despite all development efforts—not even one country was able to graduate from this group to a higher income level, may be with the exception of Botswana.

Meanwhile, poverty reduction has generated its own history. This programme has covered a wide range of approaches starting from the World Banks's small-farmers-strategies in the 1970s via the costly structural adjustment policies of the 1980s to the recent poverty reduction strategies of the 1990s. Once more, the next development decade (2000-2010) has written "Attacking Poverty" on its banner. It seems that something must have gone wrong along the way. What (bitter?) lessons have been learnt from previous experience? Have they been factored into the new set of policies? Were there possibly some fundamental flaws which were overlooked, and can better results be expected during the next period? Or do the many failures and disappointments demonstrate that there is some systemic "resistance to change" by those in power in the least developed countries and perhaps also by the poor themselves?

1. What can the Rural Poor Really Expect from Poverty Reduction Programmes?

In India, of example, 70 per cent of the people still earn their livelihood in the agricultural sector; most of the poor among them live in a kind of rural subsistence economy. People who live in a subsistence economy are naturally conservative. They are busy securing their survival and are very reluctant to take risks. Their living standard is measured in amounts of rice harvested; their wealth is measured in numbers of livestock. Within this simple framework, poor peasants behave very rationally. For example, a shift from food crops to cash crops, such as from rice to coffee or tapioca, would immediately endanger their subsistence in case of failure. Furthermore, the poor do not have the knowledge and skills to change their crops quickly in response to market demands. Moving from a subsistence economy to a commodity economy is therefore a big step for small farmers.

However, poor people are always happy to receive handouts from the Government like fertilizer, seeds, medicine or blankets. Roads, bridges and schools are also very welcome. Who would refuse a gift? From their point of view, it is the responsibility of the Government to distribute goods and services in form of aid programmes as a way to share some of the prosperity of the city people with them. Nevertheless, as they see no direct and immediate benefit for themselves, they tend to take a rather passive attitude to change. Development workers have often complained about this common apathy and about the lack of will among the poor themselves to improve their situation. In the final analysis, rural development is more a problem of providing the right economic incentives for change than of overcoming traditional thinking and a conservative attitude.

2. What Kind of Incentives are Necessary to Achieve Increased Production in the Countryside?

In most poor countries the key to rural development is the problem of land ownership rights and of legal security. As long as people do not own the land that they cultivate, they are not interested in making any investments, be they in the form of labour or capital. Once a farmer has an ownership title and considers the land as his own, he will refrain from overusing the soil but shift crops and plant new trees. Moreover, he can then use his land as collateral for credits or even sell it and buy land somewhere else.

In addition to clear and irrevocable ownership rights, the rule of law is another crucial factor for development. People must feel safe from abuse of power by local elites and corrupt government officials. They must be able to enforce their basic rights in an impartial court of law. Furthermore, they must be safe from land expropriation without adequate compensation and from resettlement against their will. In other words, it is primarily their very stake holdership in the rural economy that will motivate them to increase their production. Of course, the other necessary incentives are access to markets, a fair price for their products and the availability of goods and services.

3. Poverty Reduction Programmes, if not Accompanied by Parallel Institutional Reforms, Run the Risk of Creating a Modern Version of the Cargo Cult

Cargo cults spread during World War II in the highlands of Papua New Guinea at a time when several US cargo planes loaded with food supplies crashed into the hills. Suddenly, the native people could enjoy an abundant amount of goods, which literally fell down on them like a "gift from heaven". In the hope of attracting some more of these "silvery birds", the local hill tribes constructed primitive models of airplanes, sat around them in a circle, and prayed that more "cargo" would drop on their territory. As this happened in some areas (albeit as a result of the air battle between Japan and the USA), it strengthened the belief in the cargo cult as some magical way to overcome poverty, at least for a short time.

There is a high risk that aid programmes under the banner of poverty reduction will create new "cargo cults" in the 49 least developed countries if they continue to carry out their "business as usual" and do not put strong emphasis on the rule of law and civil rights. Unfortunately, the setting up of reliable legal and social institutions in poor countries (which often seems to be the "software" of the development industry accompanying disbursements) is, in fact, as decades of experience have shown, the hard part of the process. But it is also indispensable for achieving any tangible results.

Why have there been until now only modest results in the areas of land reform, rule of law and the guarantee of basic civil rights? Why have people's participation and people's ownership as a strategy hardly taken root at all in the least developed countries? The answer must be sought in the role of powerful local groups and their vested interest who obviously benefit from the prevailing status quo and a loose legal environment. A cargo cult promises bounty for all recipients; poverty reduction, however, means changing the rural power structure, too.

Conclusion

To insist on the rule of law, on people's participation in the development process and on transparency and accountability, is again nothing new. Good political and administrative institutions go hand in hand with economic growth. The potential of economic development is quite limited if it works in a framework of social undevelopment and official indifference. Again the question is, who has so little been achieved in this field during previous decades? Was it the wrong medicine and why were the poor results of the aid programmes so carefully ignored by the international donor community?

Looking at the political systems of the 49 least devèloped countries, it is obvious that most of these countries are "more democratic in principle than in practice". Many of them are ruled by military or civil authoritarian regimes which are more used to giving orders than to listening to the grievances of the poor, Other governments, such as India, are "genuinely democratic at most levels but have historically found it difficult that political accountability reaches all levels of decision-making, particularly for the poor."

To sum up, it seems that resistance to change is equally shared by the cumbersome and often incompetent bureaucracies of the poor countries and the equally cumbersome international donor community, which has so far conveniently kept the call for more rural democracy and people's rights on the backburner. The major reason for the reluctance of the donor community to pursue the battle for the rule of law and the fight against endemic corruption was to avoid massive political confrontation with the receiver countries.

Would it not have been better to create proper incentives for the performance of poor countries, namely by halting loans to nations that do not manage their economies and their reform commitments effectively and increasing financial and technical support to those that do? The next decade will show how determined both local governments and donors are to tackle these problems for the sake of a better future.

29

Unemployment in the Poor and Rich Worlds

Different Causes, but Converging Policies?

In view of the magnitude of global unemployment, all the customary formulas offered by economists against mass unemployment—the basic socio-economic problem of modern times—appear to be quackery. Neither quantitative, nor any kin of 'qualitative', growth will be able to eliminate the disastrous worldwide lack of jobs. For ecological reasons it is impossible to include 800 million or more unemployed in the production process through corresponding growth. The resulting increase in global Gross Domestic Product would require consumption of natural resources, energy and the environment which, given even the greatest possible productivity in those sectors, could not even be sustained for two or three decades.

In addition, aiming to achieve full employment through growth will be ever more difficult even in the rich economies. For it is most likely that work productivity will continue to rise worldwide. Countries such as China, which are in the initial phase of modernisation, are still producing at a relatively still low productivity rate. But that is precisely why they can achieve notable increases in productivity in a short time by importing technology from highly-developed countries. The advantage of rapid 'catch-up rationalisation', however , is being bought at the cost of rising unemployment and progressive impoverishment.

Employment Through Redistribution of Work

The notion that jobs can at some time be created for 800-900 million unemployed who will work 35 or even 40 hours a week at the productivity level of the highly-developed countries of four or five decades ago is absurd. The only realistic possibility of eliminating the world's unemployment problem is by far-reaching redistribution of work and income. The change needed for that demands fundamentally new concepts of prosperity: a reflection on the philosophy of the 'life of happiness'. 'New concepts of prosperity' means that technological progress would no longer be used mainly to deliver rising per capita incomes and excessive consumption. Instead, given a sufficient material standard of living, the quality of life would be improved primarily by shortening working hours. It is about, so to speak, assigning instrumental good sense new goals. Plus reshaping socio-economic conditions in such a way that the politicians will again be compelled to orient themselves on the good of the community and humanistic values instead of filling the pockets of the wealthy. It is sheer ideology, although very persuasive, to cite 'globalisation' and its alleged 'iron laws' in defaming the welfare state, full employment and social justice as out-of-date wishful thinking. A return to the state-guided social competitive system as practised during the first decades after the Second World War is possible just as it was politically feasible to make the transition from the old order of unfettered, ruthless capitalism to the mixed economies of the social market economy types. So it is a matter of restoring the proven structures of a mixed economic system.

However, in contrast to the first post war decades it is now not sufficient to regenerate nation-sate interventionism. Appropriate international regualtions are required. Above all, it will depend upon reversing the new laissez-faire developments in international economic relationships which today are subsumed under the buzzword 'globalisation'. That is, to oppose over-liberalisation and its disastrous social and inhuman impacts. It will depend on the broad mobilisation of the losers in the process of globalisation whether the necessary fundamental change of course can still be made in time before a catastrophe. In particular, the new myth must be opposed that declares globalisation as a kind of law of nature and thus suggests resignation and adaptation to an allegedly unavoidable process of destruction of social and human achievements.

Mass Unemployment in the Poor Economies

The employment problems in the rich and the poor hemispheres differ not only in their magnitude, but also in their causes. The wretched condition of the poor economies is due above all to historical reasons: colonialism and, in the post-colonial era, the constraints to independent development imposed by the hegemonic influence of the rich industrial states. The waste of scarce resources by international and civil wars, and the dictatorships with their upperclass luxury consumption and inefficient, thus development—obstructing exploitation structures—often supported by the industrialised nations—have for a long time repressed and in many cases destroyed autonomous development potential. The colonial and post-colonial distortion also contributed at least indirectly to the current population problems of the poor countries. The politically inflicted mass poverty and under-development stabilised or in fact brought about economic, socio-psychological and ideological mechanisms which oppose an effective population policy. As we know, the average educational level in many developing countries, especially among women, is too low to give a modern population policy a chance of success. Mass unemployment in the poor countries is the result of poverty. In this respect, it is about a production-side problem: too few resources, too little real and human capital and the inefficient, unproductive use of much of the anyway limited added value of society. The picture is totally different in the rich countries—the over-production economies.

Unemployment in Over-Production Systems

The main cause of mass unemployment in the industrialised nations has nothing to do with shortages. It is a phenomenon of surplus. Greater possibilities of production can no longer be used 'sufficiently profitably because the required demand is lacking. Production is done for profit. The necessary collateral condition is the satisfying of consumer needs. Employment is not even such a condition, but only a side effect which lapses immediately when labour-free production is technically possible. Thus, national income must be shared among wages and profits (or income from property). Profit is the difference between earnings and costs. Earnings depend upon demand. Macroeconomic costs consist mainly of wages and salaries (including social security contributions). These definitive connections mean that profit can be made only if overall demand is greater than the total cost of labour. But in the final analysis this demand can only come from the profit-earners themselves. In his book, A Treatise on Money, Keynes described this nexus as the theory of the Widow's Cruse. Under capitalistic conditions, labour is only sought or hired if profit can be earned with it. But as making a profit depends upon the demand for consumption and investment by the shareholders, it can be seen that the degree of employment is determined by the demand behaviour of the class that receives income from property. In this respect, the widespread belief that greater investment also leads to more employment, namely, via the effect of investment in demand, is right.

Lower Wages Mean Lower Demand

The lower the level of wages and given an unchanged total demand, the greater are the profits that can be made. But it is more likely that in the case of falling wages the overall demand will also drop. For stabilising total demand would require the recipients of income from property to increase their spending on consumption and/or investment to the degree to which wages and the consumption based on them fell.

During the last 10 to 15 years the development of profits in most industrialised nations has been very favourable. But profits would have grown more strongly if the demand of the shareholder had been much greater. This would have created more employment at the same time. Thus, it can be assumed that the profits are simply too high for the shareholders to be able to go in for meaningful consumption or make profitable investments. That is the reason for the extreme redirection of capital from fixed assets to portfolio investment. The growth of speculative (unproductive) financial transactions during the 1980s and 1990s (buzzword: casino capitalism), corresponded with a relatively weak formation of real capital.

Wage rises, of course, narrow the scope for profit. But precisely this effect stimulated efforts to improve the profit situation not only by investment in rationalisation, but also by investment in expansion aimed at the growing mass purchasing power. Since more is being invested, the profit mass also is growing according to the principle of the Widow's Cruse. Too low wages, as it were, relieve the shareholders of the pressure to innovate and invest and allow them to earn their profits too easily. That is the real message of the 'purchasing power theory' of wages.

Over-Accumulation and Under-Consumption

Overproduction has two different causes which, however, mostly occur in tandem. They are over-investment, or creation of over-capacities, on the one hand, and lack of demand due to relative saturation and an absence of mass purchasing power on the other. But the main reason for mass unemployment in the rich hemisphere currently lies on the demand side. During the first three decades after the Second World War supply and demand rose in relative balance. Economic fluctuations showed up as temporary declines in generally positive GDP growth rates. These decades of (dynamic) balance of growth are often described today as the era of 'Fordism'. Its essential feature is that rising wages ensure continuing growth of consumption, so that equally growing profits also flow relatively continuously into investments to expand capacity and create jobs. The label

'Fordism' expresses the 'simple' view of the theory of the buying power of wages which is said to have been propagated by Henry Ford I. This was that his workers should earn enough to be able to buy the cars they made.

The astonishingly balanced development of supply and demand from 1950 to the mid-1970s was due above all to post war reconstruction and the pent-up demand of consumers who were starved by wartime economy shortages. This stimulated positive investment sentiment, and high investments brought at the same time high profits. The post war growth that led within a short time to full employment was also linked with growth in productivity, which on multi-year average was more than twice that of the crisis period of the last 25 years. Thus, the so-called employment threshold (the GDP growth rate point at which employment growth begins) was much higher in those days than it is now, although there was full employment over a longer period. This simple fact opposes the thesis often propounded today that mass unemployment is above all related to rationalisation. It is not rationalisation per se, that is, progress that boosts productivity, which is the evil. The problem is that the mistakes in distribution policy which are rooted in capitalistic structures result in increases in supply encountering insufficient demand for goods, whereby the demand for labour drops. However, the fact that demand policy contradicts the requirements of a social ethic that is ecologically responsible and right for the interests of the poor countries was already spelled out. So if a demand-oriented growth policy is practised at all, it should be designed to be as environmentally compatible as possible. After all, there are possibilities for that, such as by expanding the production of services that spare resources. A one-hour driving lesson costs more energy than one hour of ballet instruction.

The politically initiated and implemented over-liberalisation and surrender of social prosperity to global competition since the 1970s, which reproduces the old self-destructive mechanism of laissez faire, have during the last two decades markedly accelerated the crisis development inherent in the system.

Summing Up, it is noted that

- Full employments in the rich economies would certainly be possible by means of demand policy, but only at a high cost to the environment that is concomitant with high growth rates;
- The growth policy of the rich countries impairs the poor economies' possibilities of medium to long-term growth, since these are falling back ever further in the competition for ever scarcer and thus ever more expensive resources;
- The environmental collapse currently expected for the third or fourth generation after us, which obviously also will trigger a collapse of the world economy and—probably ahead of that—armed conflicts which today are hardly imaginable, would happen very much sooner if economic growth were to be increased to such a degree that it would bring full employment worldwide;
- In the long term, the problem of global unemployment and global poverty can only be solved by a policy of massive redistribution, and in fact a redistribution of work and income, whereby increases in productivity must be used mainly or only for shortening working hours. That is a demand, which appears to be utopian. But utopias of today often have the quality of scripting the reality of tomorrow.

30

Solving the Unemployment Problem by Looking Beyond the Job

If you had a job, you worked; if you didn't, you didn't. Having a job meant being employed by an organisation in a clearly defined and stable occupational role, with duties, hours, rates of pay and promotion all more or less standardized. But the job—in that meaning of the world—is a social invention and a fairly recent one.

The job—the kind that you had, or hoped to get—became a central fixture of life. Its importance was great because it served many needs: For managers and efficiency experts, job assignments were the key to assembly-line manufacturing. For union organisers, jobs protected the rights of workers. For political reformers, standardized civil service positions were the essence of good government. Jobs provided an identify to immigrants and recently urbanised farm workers. They provided a sense of security for individuals and an organising principle for society.

Jobs functioned in so many ways that it is surprising how many organisations are now opting for other ways to define and manage work. The second job shift is underway. Its emergence can be seen in the increasing use of temporary and part-time workers and contracted-out services, the changing relationships between workers and management, the growing popularity of self-employment and small business. Indeed, "de-jobbing" is proceeding at such a pace that many economists, management experts and futurists are now talking freely about the end of the job. Bridges predicts that the job as we now know it will disappear entirely—replaced by new kinds of flexible work assignments in post-job organisations—and be remembered only as a quaint artifact of the industrial age.

One reason for the change in work is the economic rules of the survival game among organisations that employ workers. To stay successful in today's hitech consumer economy, businesses have had to re-model themselves into what some experts call "agile companies"—ones that are able to respond quickly to conditions in ever-changing fragmenting, competitive markets.

The "knowledge worker", whose work involves not simply doing something, but also applying theoretical or analytical skills. Such workers are replacing the industrial labourer as the dominant part of the workforce—and their productive activities are likely to be organised and structured much differently from those of their assembly-line predecessors.

De-jobbing as a result of new technology or the emergence of a service economy is a phenomenon that gets a lot of attention these days; but it is not the whole story. At all levels of society, people are improvising livelihoods that do not fit the industrial-era model. Immigrants to the developed countries, often unable to find steady jobs, nevertheless find places in the new landscape by being mobile, flexible, resourceful and imaginative: they moonlight, work part-time, share jobs, start small businesses. Their lives are often extremely difficult, but they are also instructive to those of us who believe you either have a job or you're out of luck.

It is too early to evaluate the implications of this multifaceted transformation of work, or to dismiss it as simply good or bad. Nevertheless, one cannot deny that it is taking place and will bring about dramatic social changes.

On the downside, the job shift is causing great hardships for many workers and their families. It poses serious challenges to policy-makers, political activists and labour leaders. The basic question appears to be whether the key to global employment-development strategy is to play "catch-up"—trying to bring millions of people around the world into jobs in industries and the public sector; or to play "leapfrog"—creating new forms of employment.

The proposal to generate more employment in agriculture, for example, is based on new demand for agricultural exports from developing countries. The policies designed to make the most of this opportunity include measures to upgrade technology, raise productivity, ensure the supply of essential inputs, establish marketing and distribution channels, create links between agriculture and industry and cater to export markets.

The issue of part-time work, another kind of employment that is seriously undervalued in the traditional industrial era job mind-set. Part-time work may not offer much at this point to developing countries, where many people are under employed and wages are low, but it can be of great help in more advanced economies. And it is likely to be a big part of the global work picture in the years ahead.

A certain agility may also be necessary in agriculture, particularly in countries that for many years have depended heavily on producing commodities such as sugar for export as a means of generating income and employment. As Northern laboratories develop non-agricultural substitutes for many of these commodities—and this is already beginning to happen—the bottom may fall out of "monoculture" economies, only economic, but will have long-run political implications as communities attempt to reorganise themselves in response to the changed conditions. It is, therefore, in the interest of raw materials exporters to closely monitor current trends in biotechnology and the use of genetic resources and modify their internal policies in anticipation of potential long-term effects.

This calls for flexibility and an ability to get information and to act on it. Government officials, development workers, community leaders and individuals will, in some respects, all have to be "knowledge workers" if they are to keep ahead of global changes. Jobs are going to be created not just by putting people to work, but by finding—or creating—new niches where they can be productive.

It is still possible to talk about jobs for all, and to resist the assumption made by many economists that high levels of unemployment are now inevitable. But, as we move ahead into the global information economy, we may be moving back into an older conception of the job, and seeing it again as something you do, rather than as something you have—or that has you.

31

Policy Researchers and Policy Makers

Never the Twain Shall Meet?

In every corner of the planet, researchers are gathering and analysing information on vital issues of sustainable development. But how do they know that their findings will actually be used in policy decisions that create positive change? Researchers and decision makers see the world, and their roles in it, in very different ways. What creates this divide between the two communities and what can be done to bridge the gap?

Demand-Side' Challenges: Policy in the Making

By its nature, the policy making process constrains decision makers from effectively expressing demands for research. Rigorous research requires a clear definition of a problem and the variables to be measured. But the objectives of government policies and programmes tend to be loosely defined and even contradictory. Many decisions are reached through a multilateral bargaining process in which it is difficult to obtain consensus on anything more than broad statements of principle. These bargains might break down if the costs and tradeoffs involved were exposed by a research project.

Inertia and more urgent priorities mean that government tend to think about changing policies only when time and funding have run out. At that point, it is too late for research. Furthermore, it is only after a programme has been established and a clientele created that an effective demand exists for research. For these reasons, policy implementation tends to precede rather than follow research.

Even if there is a need for research, there may not be a single agency responsible for the policy decision bargaining. When a client agency does request advice, there is no guarantee that it will turn out to be the appropriate audience for the results (e.g. a study done for the ministry of education might find that student performance would be improved by better nutrition).

Finally, governments are often afflicted with too much information, which senior policy makers have little time to absorb.

'Supply Side' Challenges of Academic Research

Problems also exist in the research community that supplies information and analysis. University research usually takes a long time to yield results. It is often highly critical, without suggestions for action, but fitting the self-image of many academics a gadflies. In academia, a state of conflicting views and information is normal. But potential clients find their confidence undermined when two studies reach opposite conclusions.

Academics often search for general laws and patterns that reveal phenomena of greater theoretical and long run importance than highly specific observations. Policy makers, however, want answers to the specific problems they face, even if such 'small' problems do not interest researchers.

While policy makers tend to emphasise distributional concerns (i.e. winners and losers) and the number of people affected, economists—frequent advisors to government—emphasise efficiency and financial costs and benefits. Owing partly to the vagueness of many programme goal, policy makers tend to assess performance in terms of inputs rather than improvements in health. They also weigh losses more heavily than gains, since "a policy that hurts five people and helps five, produces five enemies and five ingrates".

Finally, the issue of compensation is critical to policy makers; for economists it is usually an afterthought. Economists tend to find a solution satisfactory if, in theory, the losers could be compensated. To push a policy change through, policy makers must usually ensure that they will be compensated and have mechanisms to do so.

Impact Down the Road

The gap between demand and supply for research appears rather large. But this view may be too pessimistic, mainly because it uses narrow definitions of research and policy impact. Research is more than a set of data and policy impact may accumulate imperceptibly but with real effect over many years. The contribution of social science research is perhaps less in proposing specific solutions to well-defined problems, than in defining the problems and providing an array of concepts and methods for analysis.

Problem definition can take many forms. It can mean detecting problems from patterns in data, such as a trend toward worsening income distribution. It can also change the way society thinks about issues. Largely because of research, the informal sector now tends to be seen as a potential force for development, rather than a symptom of backwardness.

The most significant contribution of social science research may be in generating ideas and ideologies, which history shows can be very powerful.

What to do?

How, then, can researchers and the agencies that sponsor them increase the social relevance and impact of research? Since both the problem-solving and the conceptual impacts are important, research programmes should be designed to provide both by developing an understanding of basic behavioural relationships and a thorough knowledge of the data. This can then be tapped to provide short-term policy advice.

Donors have an important role to play in supporting theoretical research, although they are sometimes reluctant to do so. The distinction between "theoretical" and "empirical" is in no sense equivalent to "useless" and "useful". A plausible, verifiable theory about how farmers respond to increases in crop prices, or savings to changes in interest rates, is of obvious relevance to poverty and can be very useful.

Greater attention should go to publicising findings and donors should be prepared to finance conferences, books, working papers, abstracts and the like. Researchers should convey their findings in language intelligible to practitioners, putting themselves into policy makers' shoes when doing so. Among the recommendations made by successful policy advisors are the following

- learn about the history of the issue by researching previous arguments, interest groups, areas of disagreement and data gaps;
- get into the debate early before positions harden;
- explain which groups will be affected by the proposed measures and suggest ways to compensate those negatively affected;
- do not propose measures that are technically optimal but too complex or costly for an agency to administer; and
- keep it simple. Emphasise the decision at hand, the underlying problem and options to solve it. Minimise methodology, jargon and equations.

In the research domain, there is no single recipe for policy impact. Luck and persistence, along with good science, are vital ingredients.

32

The Dematerialisation of the World Economy

The first Industrial Revolution marked the transition from robber-and-plunder colonialism to the systematic development of the "overseas" territories in the framework of an international division of labour between raw materials suppliers and manufacturers of finished goods. There was an "historic integration" of the colonised areas in the development of their parent—states. What will the third Industrial Revolution do for the Third World ? Will it now come to an "historic separation" ?

The end of the East-West conflict was reason enough to talk about a radical change in world politics. But at the same time an upheaval in the world economy is taking place that possibly will have even wider impacts. As a reference point for the following thoughts, three dimensions of this change are pointed out:

1 the upgrading of processing information rather than materials as object of economic activity (technological dimension);

2 the evolvement of global communications networks (socio-cultural dimension);

3 the change of the nature of work (socio-economic dimension).

All three dimensions can be summarised under the buzzphrase "tertialisation of the world economy."

In that respect, talk of the "Third Industrial Revolution" is misleading. It is not about a third epoch of industrialisation, but about the beginning of a de-industrialisation, the transition from the industrial to the information society.

Historic Separation?

In the 1960s and early 1970s, there was often talk of the Third World as the Third Sector of the world economy. Also then the Third World was not much more than an "imaginary community". But as such it had a certain significance in world politics. This implied not only its strategic role in the East-West conflict and its ideological function as the supporter of different "third paths" between capitalism and socialism. It was also about the Third World's attested "chaos power". That linked the fear (in the North) and the hope (in the South) that the developing countries would be in a position to cut off the industrial nations from supplies of important raw materials, thus putting them under pressure. But it was soon seen that both sides had over estimated this possibility, even with regard to oil. Instead of supply bottlenecks arising, raw materials prices plummeted. For some commodities, the fall in prices exceeded those of the Great Depression of 1929/30.

This was due, inter alia, to the conjunction of lower demand from the industrial nations and expansion of production by the raw materials suppliers. Business activities dependent upon the supply of raw materials are tending to lose importance compared with the overall development of the global economy. The reason for this is to be seen in the transition from a material to an information economy.

This transition is taking place in line with the revolutionising of data transmission and the expansion of financial transactions which are not directly related to changes in the production of materials. The speed of the changes is remarkable.

However, the dematerialisation of business activities does not lead to decoupling of the Third World from the world economy. Declining market shares in world trade are not the expression of separation, but a loss of the affected countries positions in the world economy. Thus, the impact of dematerialisation is "only" that the negotiating positions of raw materials suppliers vis–a–vis the industrial nations will deteriorate further.

Differentiation of the Third World

But the radical change in the global economy is affecting some developing countries worse than others. Sub-saharan Africa and some countries in West and South Asia and Latin America are being pushed back further. The oil-producing countries with their high per capita export earnings will be able to hold their positions in the world economy for some time to come. The threshold countries of East and South-East Asia can expand theirs so long as they can continue to attract a growing share of global industrial production, and at the same time participate in the tertialisation of the world economy in the shape of rapidly-growing financial transactions. Thereby it should be noted that the degree of tertialisation in itself is not an adequate indicator for economic avant-gardism. Brazil exhibits a high degree of tertialisation in combination with a low macro-economic development dynamics. A good part of its tertialisation is being achieved by speculative financial transactions with their inherently greater risks and uncertainties than in the industrial countries. Such dangers have been demonstrated by Mexico's peso crisis and its repercussions on the whole of Latin America.

In some Third World countries, a "location annuity" has replaced the old raw materials one. Here it's about providing locations for off-shore transactions which offer international capital traders a maximum of freedom of movement combined with low taxation. Suitable for such operations are small countries which, despite low levy rates, achieve significant income in macro-economic terms.

The radical changes in the world economy are spurring the differentiation of the Third World without, however, necessarily fostering a dissolution of the Third World as an "imaginary community". It is precisely the advanced countries of East and South-East Asia that are showing a certain interest in the formulation of joint positions of the "South" in order to secure their own positional gains in the global economy. It's not by chance that the non-aligned countries and the Group of 77 have formed a joint coordination committee, and that the ASEAN countries are changing course on the international human rights policy.

Hitherto, the developing countries' strategy was to broaden the concept of human rights as a justification for demands on the industrial nations. But of late some developing countries, led by the ASEAN states, have questioned the universal validity of human rights even after their universality was confirmed by consensus at the Conference on Human Rights in Vienna in 1993. Playing a role in this policy is the governments' fear that due to the expansion of global communications networks, the behaviour patterns and preferences of their own people could in some way become similar to those of the West. As the rulers see it, that would be detrimental to the continuation of the development models practised so far.

Internet Creates New Cultural Dimension

Much information which Asian governments view as subversive in already globally available on the Internet. The old struggle over the world information order, which at first was primarily a clinch between East and West, is thus taking on a new dimension. For with the growing importance of computer literacy to a country's ability to assert itself on world markets, the Asian threshold countries have not only an interest in controlling the on-line communication but also to expand it and the know-how that it requires.

Even the critics of any interventions in the internet and other global communications networks must admit that modern communications technologies are politically blind and their use in itself does not represent progress. The setting up and expansion of global information highways will offer forum not only to people who want to use it for education and enlightenment, but also to all shades of fundamentalists. These highways will not necessarily bring the misery of many Third World regions closer to the industrial countries, but possibly rather strengthen the tendency to process all world events as entertainment.

Global Two-thirds Society

The gravest aspect of the current upheaval in the world economy is its negative impact on jobs. The information economy needs for fewer workers than an economy based on materials. Instead, the demands on the skills of the workers are growing. Twenty per cent of the world workforce will in future be employed as (overworked) "intelligence workers". Eighty per cent will work part–time, if they are not underemployed or jobless. So the tertialisation of the global economy delivers more underemployment rather than more leisure time. The workers who are rationalised out of their jobs in the industrial sector cannot be absorbed by the service sector because it, too, is not left untouched by rationalisation measures. The civil service is also cutting back on staff. At all levels, there's a race to make the greatest possible savings on payrolls. At the same time, there's growing pressure to cut costs in providing for the victims of this development. That means thinning out the social security safety net.

The bottom line is that the two-thirds society, which developmental action groups hitherto assumed was limited to the Third World, is spreading worldwide. That, however, will not in the foreseeable future lead to an amendment of the North-South disparities. It's true that the change in the global economy is taking place faster, and to a greater extent in the industrial nations. But rationalisation is also happening in the developing countries in a bid to boost their competitiveness. So the upheaval in the world economy aggravates the problems which exist in a majority of the developing countries, while creating new ones in the industrial nations. The need for action on the North-South policy is growing, among the industrial nations. The need for action on the North-South Policy is growing, while the industrial nations' scope for concessions and compromises is shrinking. The new social question which is now crystallizing at global level is not being answered. The consequences are unforeseeable.

Another Loser?

It's more probable that a sharpening of the North–South confrontation is to be reckoned with. For the industrial nations will attempt to keep the social costs of the information economy at bay for as long as possible. The trade unions will thereby compete with the developing countries for jobs for their members. But this policy has its limits precisely because of the peaking of the problems in the industrial nations. Overstepping these limits means war and passively accepting them chaos and social decay. Solutions could be sought in two directions: effective taxation of the information economies and the creation of jobs in the non-profit sector. But it's possible there are no global solutions for global problems. That would mean for at least part of the Third World a renewal of the old debate on partial decoupling from the world economy.

33

A New World Order for Whom?

"Four holocausts" humanity has produced are breeding the seeds of our own destruction: war and militarisation, human oppression, economic destitution and environmental destruction. The "new world orders" on offer can satisfy only the minority of the world's rich and will ultimately only exacerbate these four trends towards global annihilation. But there is also hope in the "grassroots world order" leading to the civil society, democratisation and social mobilisation as the only way for the planet to survive.

As we approach the end of the 20th century and a new millennium, humanity is faced with four conditions of its own making, so serious in terms of their present destruction of life and risks for the future that they warrant a description as "four holocausts".

The *first* holocaust is that of war and militarisation. After the Gulf War it is clear that, far from preparing the way for world peace, that conflict has unleashed a new global arms race in the weapons whose brutal effectiveness was so clearly demonstrated in Iraq. The *second* holocaust is that of human oppression, the violent denial by governments of the basic personal, civil, political and economic rights of their citizens, which routinely persist in a majority of countries of the world. The *third* holocaust is that of economic destitution, the mass poverty of a fifth of the world's population, leading to endemic malnutrition, disease and death, not least among children. And the *fourth* holocaust is that of environmental destruction, which is gradually or not so gradually rendering the planet uninhabitable, as witnessed by the growing millions of environmental refugees whose bankrupt ecosystems can no longer support them.

None of these circumstances is entirely new to our age, of course, war, repression, destitution and ecological degradation have often been part of the human condition. What is new about the current situation is its global nature. All humanity, the whole earth, is now at risk. And it is all humanity which must be party to a response, if it is to be successful.

Against this threatening background, several new developments stand out. First, is the collapse of communism, taking out of the bounds of credibility socialism's millenarian dream of abolishing the market and inevitably replacing capitalism through the onward march of history. Second, there are the twin trends of globalisation and interdependence: globalisation especially of the economy, interdependence especially through environmental impacts. This is the context for any discussion of a "new world order".

The New World Orders

There are, broadly, three kinds of new world orders currently on offer. The real world is almost certainly going to be mixture of all three, but the balance between them will be crucial in deciding whether we will successfully manage to face and overcome, the holocausts raging among us.

The first kind of new world order may be called the "neoliberal". Its most important component is the untrammelled operation of what we would call the global "free market". At once we must qualify this terminology by noting that the freedom bestowed on someone by the market is in direct proportion to the amount of property owned by that person within it. In a free market, those who own the means of production are free to produce what, when and where they want, and largely to determine the conditions of production. Those who own the means of consumption can similarly scour the world for products to satisfy their wants. The extent to which this "freedom" is far from universal is shown by the fact that, with regard to consumption some 23 per cent of the world's population control 85 per cent of the income which is consumptions prerequisite and ownership of the means of production is more concentrated still. The neoliberal world order thus represents a good deal for perhaps a quarter of the world's population, but has precious little to offer the rest.

A Global Order Framed by International Institutions

The second kind of new world order may be termed the "social democratic" and is roughly that advocated in the 1970's by the proponents of a New International Economic Order. These two new world orders clearly different but they also share several characteristics which seem to be more significant than their differences. First, they are explicitly western-oriented and homogenizing. They view the world through the eyes of western science and western culture simultaneously devaluing the knowledge and accumulated wisdom of the great majority of human kind. The paradigm society, towards which all others are supposed to be developing or aspiring to develop, is that of the United States.

Second, both these world orders are economistic. Human progress and development to them means economic developments, still usually measured by the level and growth of GNP per person. No social or cultural tradition or aspiration is allowed to stand in the way of this "development". Third, both world views envisage top-down decision-making for administration and control. For the neoliberals the dominant influence is exercised by the owners and managers of transnational capital. For the social democrats their influence is balanced by the interventions of international and national bureaucrats. Neither world order places great store on consultation with, let alone decision-making by, ordinary people in their communities.

In contrast to these two new world orders, it is possible to posit a third, here called the grassroots new world order, which takes as its principal focus neither the market nor the state (national or international), but civil society, the networks of family, community and voluntary association acting for social reproduction, reconstruction or reform. This new world order has characteristics diametrically opposed to those shared by the first two discussed. Its impulse derives explicitly from the bottom up, drawing on the capability and creativity of those united by shared values and interests, at the local level or in wider networks. Their world-view is one of cultural diversity, of one world comprised many different villages rather than a homogeneous global village modelled on the US. They perceive human development to be holistic, with the economic dimension integrated with, or embedded in, a broader social, ethical and ecological reality. And they proceed from an ethical basis that strives for ecological sustainability, social justice in distribution and broad participation in cultural, political and economic life.

Looking to the Grassroots World Order

After this thumbnail sketch of these three views of different dominant global processes, one can ask which of them or, more realistically, what balance between them, will be best able to put an end to the four holocausts tormenting humanity. There is only one convincing answer: the dominant thrust must be towards the grassroots new world order. There are several reasons for this. Most obviously, it is indisputable that it is the forces of the market and the state that have not only failed to douse, but have actually fanned the flames of all four holocausts. It states that go to war and waste the commonwealth on weaponry. It states that are responsible for the great majority of violence and repression against ordinary people. It states, often supported by multilateral governmental organisations such as the World Bank and IMF, that have the so called Third World intervened massively in the subsistence, largely non-market economies of the people and redistributed their resources, redefining their very rights to property, in favour of industrialisation and market exchange. But these enhanced markets have then spectacularly failed to provide alternative subsistence for those dispossessed, leaving them by the million impoverished, marginalised and destitute. Moreover, this process has set in train two great engines of environmental destruction: industrialisation itself, with its toxic pollution, soil erosion, water and ozone depletion and climate destabilisation; and the depredations of the rural dispossessed, forced into forests or onto marginal lands, deforesting, making deserts, extinguishing species and multiplying in numbers in their desperate efforts to stay alive.

Civil Society Mobilising for Human Survival

In contrast, it is civil society that has mobilised explicitly against the four holocausts. The great social movements of our time are those for peace and human rights, for justice and development and for environmental conservation. It is independent, non-violent associations of civil society that have sought explicitly to address these issues, meeting at best indifference from organisations of the market and the state, at worst outright hostility.

This is not at all to say that the market and state are irredeemable, or that they have no role in combating the four holocausts of destruction. On the contrary, they each have a vital contribution to make but, it order to make it, each must first be transformed. The market failures caused by great concentrations of wealth and power, ubiquitous externalities, the tyranny of small decisions and positional goods can only be resolved by determined and democratic state action. But most governments are not democratic. On the contrary most are unrepresentative and self-serving, many are vicious and corrupt. And the only force that can democratise them is that of civil mobilisation and organisation.

Viewing the immense power of today's concentrations of wealth and the remoteness of most governments from their people, one may feel despair at the prospect of civil society being able to harness these forces to the common good. And indeed there is no certainty that they will be thus harnessed. The four holocausts may simply run their awful course. But since 1989, at least, there is proof positive in the peaceful revolutions in Eastern Europe and the Soviet Union, that civil society can overturn seemingly omnipotent despotic structures. And all over the world the various movements for peace, justice and the environment are organising for human survival. The stakes have never been so high and the outcome is uncertain; but there are legitimate and inspiring grounds for hope.

Bibliography

Anand, R.P., *Legal Regime of Sea Bed and the Developing Countries,* 1975.

Bhatt, S., *Environment Protection and International Law,* Radiant Publication, Kalkaji, New Delhi, 1985, pp. 122.

Bhatt, S., *Environmental Laws and Water Resources Management,* Radiant Publication, India and Advent Books Inc. New York, 1986, pp. 355.

Behrman, Danial, *In Partnership with Nature—UNESCO and the Environment* (Paris, 1973).

Bell, Daniel, "Technology, Nature and Society", *American Scholar,* Summer 1973.

Bentley, Glass, *"Biology and Human Values",* USIS, New Delhi.

Book of Nature. The Way Things Work, published by George Allen and Unwin Ltd., 1981, pp. 525.

Boulding, Kenneth E., "New Goals for Society", S.H. Schun, ed., *Energy, Economic Growth and the Environment.*

Carr, E.H., *What is History,* 1961.

Darlington, C.D., *The Evolution of Man and Society* (London, 1961).

Downing, Paul B., ed., *Air Pollution and Social Sciences* (New York, 1971).

"Drive to Adopt National Water Policy", *Times of India,* 22 July, 1983.

Dubos, Rene, "Man and His Environment", *Britannica Perspectives,* Vol. 1, 1968.

Einstein, A., *My Views,* ed., by S.K. Bandopadhyaya (Calcutta, 1976).

"Environment Research Programme", prepared by NCEPC, Department of Science and Technology, New Delhi.

Forbes, R.J., "The Conquest of Nature and its Consequences", *Britannica Perspectives,* Vol. 1, 1968.

Fowler, John M., *Energy and Environment* (New York, 1975).

Fuller, Buckminister, R., *Operating Manual for Spaceship Earth* (New York, 1969).

Gandhi, Indira, "Poverty Greatest Pollution, says Mrs. Gandhi", *Times of India,* 8 September, 1981.

Glenn, Seaborg, *"Science, Technology and Development: A New World Outlook",* USIS, New Delhi.

Hacoley, Amos H., *Human Ecology* (New York, 1950).

"India Must Develop Own Ecology", *Times of India,* 8 October 1981.

Marion, Jerry B., *Energy in Perspective* (London, 1974).

Misra, K.C., *Manual of Plant Ecology,* New Delhi, 1980.

Mukherji, P.K., *Life of Tagore,* Trans, by S.K. Ghosh, 1975.

Mumford, Lewis, "The Future of Cities", In *Basic Issues in Environment,* E.J. Winn, ed., 1972.

Palmslierna, H., *Future Impertives for Human Environment,* 1972.

Pavithran, A.K., "World Futurology", *Eastern Journal of International Law* (Madras), Vol. 9.

"Plans to Usher India into 21st Century", *Times of India,* 24 October, 1985.

Polunin, Nicholas, "The Biosphere Today", *The Environmental Future,* Proceedings of Ist International Conference on Environmental Future in Finland, ed. by N. Polunin, 1972.

Radhakrishnan, S., *Recovery of Faith,* 1967.

Report on the State of Environment Prepared by Centre for Science and Environment, New Delhi, 1985.

Sarkar, Mahendra Nath, *The Cultural Heritage of India,* Vol. 1.

Sen, Sudhir, "Blueprint for a Better World", *Times of India,* 2 March, 1980.

The Limits to Growth, A Report to Club of Rome (New York, 1972).

The Mind of J. Krishnamurti, ed. by L.S.R. Vas (Bombay, 1971).

Toynbee, Arnold, "Man and His Soul", *Hindustan Times,* 4 January, 1968.

United Nations List of National Parks and Protected Areas, 1985.

Vivekananda, Swami, *Complete Works,* Vol. II (Calcutta, 1968).

Ward, Barbara and Dubos Rene, *Only one Earth: The Care and Maintenance of a Small Planet,* Report to UN Conference on Human Environment, Stockholm, 1972.

"Wildlife Laws in India", *Times of India,* 4 March, 1985.

Ward, Barbara, *Progress for a Small Planet,* 1979.

INDEX